Let
Them
Write
Creatively

GRACE K. PRATT-BUTLER

Cleveland State University

CHARLES E. MERRILL PUBLISHING COMPANY
A Bell & Howell Company
Columbus, Ohio

Published by
Charles E. Merrill Publishing Company
A Bell & Howell Company
Columbus, Ohio

International Standard Book Number: 0-675-09065-2

Library of Congress Catalog Card Number: 72-83819

Printed in the United States of America

1 2 3 4 5 6 7 8—78 77 76 75 74 73

PREFACE

This short paperback on the subject of creative writing is for the use of those who work with children from age three through age twelve or from nursery school through grade six. Although very young children do not themselves write, they can and do function in creative bodily rhythms and express themselves in art media. Encouragement at this age enriches and develops creative verbal expression. Alertness on the part of the teacher in recording such expression is an important precursor to creative writing. Environmental factors can assist in creative writing. The role of the teacher is strategic in encouraging especially the outgoing, the reticent, and the non-English-speaking child. Numerous samples of children's work as well as suggestions to guide teachers are included in this book. There can be elements of creativity in the so-called practical writing of children, too.

I have taught college students planning to teach as well as many experienced teachers. I have taught children from age three through twelve for a number of years. I believe firmly that all possess the potentiality to become creative and I seek to actualize these possibilities for the children who will be taught today and in days to come. Let them write creatively is a plea and a challenge. It is one road to realization!

At this time, thanks are due to those who have been supportive and to the many children who wander through these pages in their speaking and writing. Thanks are due, too, to the schools which permitted the development of these theories and practices. Among them must be listed the following: the Midtown Ethical Culture School; the Brooklyn Ethical Culture School; the Riverside Neighborhood School; the Campus School of the New York State College for Teachers at Buffalo; a number of individual public school classes in Brooklyn and Manhattan; and Hudson Guild Settlement.

Special appreciation is expressed to the Midtown Ethical Culture School where, for many years during an earlier part of a long career,

I had the freedom to formulate and to try out a number of the ideas expressed here.

I owe a genuine debt of gratitude to the Brooklyn Ethical Culture School and to its principal, Arthur Sussman. My work as Ethics consultant there for several years became an end for which a number of creative activities served as means to the consideration of ethical problems. Although the latter are not fully recorded here, some of the creative writing techniques developed within this context are described in Chapter 5.

The many graduate and undergraduate students, known to me during my many years in various positions at the Brooklyn Center of Long Island University, served to add various insights for which gratitude is expressed. The experiences and activities of children from the public schools of New York City were a part of these years.

This little book is an expression of a philosophy of education functioning through one outlet—creative writing—and it is hoped that it will serve those who work with children from three through twelve years of age.

Grace K. Pratt-Butler

Cleveland, Ohio
June, 1972

CONTENTS

to
my beloved husband
ALAN

Let
Them
Write
Creatively

1

What Is Creativity Through Language?

*The context of creative writing;
communicating through nonverbal as
well as verbal forms of expression.*

Creative writing is a means of expression which everyone can and should enjoy in one or more of its many forms. Doesn't every educated person write? But how many can, and do, express what they genuinely feel? If they do, how many can view what has been written critically?

To what extent can we develop creative writing as a means by which children can communicate their feelings outwardly and to others?

Before considering these questions, it is necessary to set down a few premises which may be used as both clarification and definition for what is to come. In this chapter, the importance of the role of the teacher is stated and defined. No matter how creative an individual child may be, or can be, there are a few general expectations which should be held for all children as guideposts. It is up to each child to develop specific expectations in terms of himself, his group, and his teacher. To do this, he requires a teacher who is responsive to him and who realizes that *this is the child's right.*

The first step in answering these questions is to define the three major concepts: creativity, communication, and language.

CREATIVITY

The question "What is creativity?" has several possible answers. In a positive vein, one answer might be that it's "the stuff of which artists are made!" Or, more negatively, "the thing that causes misfits and recently has exploded the population of Greenwich Village." Needless to say, creativity need not make one into a misfit, nor, on the other hand, be considered only in terms of artistic talent.

Hughes Mearns[1] used to tell his classes that everyone was creative. Then he would induce each and every student to prove it before the end of the semester. As a former student of his, I recall a middle-aged woman, who insisted that she was not, never had been, and could not ever be creative. Within a week or ten days, however, she was willing to admit that she *did* trim hats! Furthermore, she devised *her own* way of doing it! Many of us remember the mother in *A Raisin in the Sun,*[2] who answered the somewhat contemptuous comment about her rather sad-looking geranium, which she planned to take when the family moved to more elegant quarters, with "This is the expression of me." Leonard, Van Deman, and Miles put this a bit differently when they state,

> Early childhood education, in making creative expression one of its goals, recognizes creativity as a basic characteristic of all human nature . . . Young children possess the quality of non-self-conscious spontaneity that creativity demands.[3]

My contention is that all of us do possess the means, both mentally and emotionally, to be creative. However, young children must be given all possible opportunity for developing it, or creativity will tend to be overwhelmed, repressed, or diverted into submission to the patterning of others. To actualize this potentiality, meager though it may be at first, is everyone's right.

Torrance stated, over ten years ago, that:

> As might be expected more varied materials and tasks have been used in assessing the creative capabilities of children during the elementary school period than during the preschool period. With

---

[1]Hughes Mearns was for many years Professor of Creative Education at New York University. See Hughes Mearns, *Creative Power*, 2nd rev. ed. (New York: Dover Publications, Inc., 1958).

[2]Lorraine Hansberry, *A Raisin in the Sun* (New York: Random House, Inc., 1959).

[3]Edith Leonard, Dorothy Van Deman, and Lillian Miles, *Foundations of Learning in Childhood Education* (Columbus, Ohio: Charles E. Merrill Books, Inc., 1963), p. 91.

increased ability to communicate ideas through speech and writing this becomes possible.[4]

While it is certainly easier, as he said, to measure and to evaluate the written answer or the spoken response, the recent upsurge of general concern about education for the preschool ages may make a difference. The worthy preschool teacher encourages the child's initial impetus to create. Once awakened, creativity, through whatever media selected, should continue to function as one dynamic force in every child. Hopefully, there will be further studies of the elementary level and greater productivity there due to preschool initiation and guidance. However, despite the lack of easy means of measurement, there has recently been a tremendous increase in the quantity of work created by preschool children. Let's not lose what we have gained! Vast numbers of preschoolers now create through various media. Let's keep them creating, not only throughout the elementary school years, but throughout their lives. While creativity may be the stuff of which artists are made, it is also a source of realization for each and every one of us. Creativity is the individual communicating, to himself and to others. What is communicated creatively is individual and unique!

COMMUNICATION

Every animal, old and young, communicates in some fashion. Communication from one to another implies imparting a sound or motion. In most natural conditions, a response is expected. Thus there is an interchange between two or more. The human baby cries and his mother responds. By the time he is able to sit in his high chair, he can utilize his spoon. His vocal, "Da, da da," is accompanied by a rhythmic banging of the spoon. It is his own means of communicating some sign of himself outward.

By the time he is in first grade, the child is confronted by a teacher who has a language arts program formulated to assist her in developing his verbal interchange. He is encouraged to speak in sentences, to listen, to read the printed word, and to comprehend what is written. Cultural demands require sentence structure, punctuation, fine grammar, and pronunciation. The child communicates—sometimes freely, more often in an imposed pattern. He can ask a question and

---

[4]E. Paul Torrance, *Guiding Creative Talent* (Englewood Cliffs, N.J.: Prentice-Hall, Inc., 1963), p. 28.

comprehend the answer given. He is beginning to read, write, and spell. If he does not develop the ability to do these things, the language arts program is revised, or he is sent to a specialist of one sort or another to investigate the reasons why he does not perform.

In the preschool, if he attended one, he manipulated materials and began to create and project himself through his block building, through dramatic play, through rhythms and rhythm band instruments, through song and chant, through paint, finger paint, and clay, and perhaps through wood and other less common media. Unfortunately, in too many cases, these were preschool activities only, although the fortunate child continues to utilize these media. Again, cultural dictates require certain music, set times, and a place for painting. In many cases, these activities are considered fine only for Saturday classes, summer camps, and play groups. Unfortunately, when this happens, the opportunities for the child to extend himself by creative expression outward through varied media are channeled. All too frequently this channeling is through ways which cut off, or seriously restrict, creativity.

All too often a child's own communication is stripped of many avenues of expression and is turned carefully toward acceptable curricular criteria, which are determined by the society's cultural objectives. The criteria may have been formulated by teachers and administrators with or without the child's cooperation. On rare occasions, the parents have had some voice. While social acceptance, social "know how," and social service are basic in any community, there should be ample opportunity also for individual creative expression. Such expression requires many varied avenues of communication so that each child has *daily* opportunity to dance, paint, or write freely in one way or another, because "I feel that way." Lacking the situations for free interchange, the child seeks empathetic respondents. Lacking these, his expression becomes a private personal source for realization. The small apartment, the crowded, overplanned day, and the noisy bustle of present life tend to mitigate against even this internal communication of the self.

Of course, children do not continue to feel and feel without additional input! A variety of both individual and group experiences using the senses should keep the inner source free so that the child continues to add to his depth and variation of feeling. For these reasons, among others, inner-city children are sometimes taken on expeditions. Some are meaningful, and they learn from them. The teacher takes the children to a zoo, a boat basin, or to a large market to extend what is meaningful. They ask questions, discuss the experience, create items from this extension of their previous experience because the zoo or market means something more now. The experience may have solved a simple problem. Are there big cats? What is a wolf? Where does Mr. Serra get his apples and oranges? The four-year-old walks like a tiger and, given musical accompaniment, he prowls silently. Later, he says, "I walked on my big tiger paws. My nails did not make a noise." Tina, a fifth grader, wrote, "She turned, and like a smooth, silent tiger, she stalked away. Her big eyes watched, and she saw back into the dark. Then, she moved back toward something in that dark." Additional experiences can feed feelings which are already present and thus may be shown in later creative expression.

Shaping the Child's Communications

I have said earlier that every child needs to communicate *freely*. As used here, *freely* means with only the fewest restrictions. Such restrictions are imposed by the limitations of the media themselves and by the rights of others. There is a distinction between freedom and license. A child who paints over the piano when old enough to realize that tempera paint is for paper and that house painting requires other materials, and a child who dances gaily over the block buildings of the other children, who scatters their books and upsets their finger painting activities, exhibits license, not freedom. The classroom is not a play therapy room, although expression—despite the few simple restrictions set—may provide necessary release and prevent the necessity for any therapy.

The child learns that the self is in a social context when in a group. Although every child is an individual, each has neither more nor less right to function as an individual than any other. The few simple rules formulated maintain the freedom of each one to communicate his expression. Interchange, yes, but abrogation of the simple rights of others, no! The various avenues of communication should remain as free as possible of obstacles. Such freedom is requisite to self and social well-being.

Creative expression takes many forms; it is like a deep pool from which flow many streams. While all have access to every stream, each person is more at ease in certain streams than in others. The various modes of expression are interrelated. While verbal forms may spring forth complete in themselves, they frequently remain either hidden or are present only in a conforming pattern. Since verbal communication follows earlier forms, through the very type of media utilized, it is frequently initially developed through a nonverbal form. Children move before they speak in coherent sentences and utter sounds before they sing. Swaying to recorded music, for instance, may bring forth,

> *Dancing, dancing down the forest green,*
> *Dancing, dancing floats the fairy queen.*

This might come from a child who would chew her pencil if asked to write her own feelings and thoughts. Creative writing is, in a sense, once removed from its creative origin, especially for the very young. One dances with one's body, and although arms and legs can be trained too, creative writing requires some special physical coordination to manipulate the external tool—the pencil on paper. It is the flow of expression, of how Petey and Polly really feel, that is the source of their creative acts. To bring this feeling forth in the form of creative writing may mean utilizing nonverbal media to stir the feelings which can also be verbalized into expression, and delaying the actual writing until coordination of finger muscles and hand-eye coordination is developed enough to hold the pencil and to write on the paper. The intermediary tool and its use should not hamper creativity. Thus the first creative "writing" may well be created by the child and recorded by a tape or the teacher. The older child, of course, does his own writing.

The result of these procedures is creative writing defined as the child's own written expression of what he really feels. Then, once it is down, his judgment may work upon it. Skills can be introduced and choices made, after the initial expression of feeling has come forth.

LANGUAGE AS MEANS AND END

Language assumes many forms and verbalization fulfills many functions. Spontaneously utilized, it is a means to communicate one's self outward, as we have seen, and it may also be a way for the self to assume a response.

When a child is creating verbally in spoken or written form, he is using language as means. Once the speech is made, the story told, the original poem written, the result is language as end. It is, in a sense, communication captured and stamped as the communicator's own. Thus it is an end for the time being. In the immediate sense, this is language as means and ends. In a more far-reaching sense, these ends function as means to future ends. The child may take his piece of writing, for instance, and utilize it as the beginning of a story. Thus language is a functional element through the means-ends continuum. All expression functions, or can function, in these ways. Bodily movement, for instance, might be another such functional element serving as means and ends in a continuum.

An example may help to clarify this. A child has an experience. He is aware of the hush of evening. He feels the quiet and is able to clarify his own feeling. He feels akin to the chirping of robins in a nearby oak. This feeling causes him to walk more softly and then to sit down, motionless, on a rock. The experience is a full one, and he feels himself responding to it. He feels so full of it that he writes,

> *The quiet evening*
> *Speaks in soft sound,*
> *As robins cease their hopping*
> *And perch in their oaks 'round*
> *Where I am stopping.*

Language, obviously, was the functional means whereby the experience, mood, and feeling were unified and externalized. Later, the poem is reread. It has become a mood objectified through language and caught as a complete act of expression. The particular experience felt by the child has been set off as a specific temporal and spatial entity. Thus it is an end. The process media is language and the end product is in written form. Thus language is end. Almost immediately it is reread and choices are made. Should the word *quiet* remain in the first line? Should the word be *dark* or *still?* Feeling, language, and critical thinking now take over as a unified force to judge and correct the poem. There is no justification for this "unified force" until the creation is there, or in other words, until the poem is written. The poem may be the first of a book of poems.

When a person communicates, he usually does one or more of the following: he makes a fact known, or gives information; he asks a question, or inquires; he describes, or tells about something; he assuages a want, or meets a need; he tries to find out, or solves a problem. As we have seen, such communication is primarily interactive. From his own inner feelings, the individual seeks to push out of himself some expression of a feeling which may or may not require an answer. However, when the feeling is expressed in an interactive way, some response is expected. I communicate how I feel to you using the words "I feel ill." On such an occasion, I do expect some response. The baby's early cry arises from a feeling of discomfort or hunger. He expresses this feeling through his own primitive language, a cry. The usual response—his mother picking him up—makes the incident an interactive one. The next cries express feeling, too, but are communicated, gradually more particularly, to his mother.

A communicator may expect no response to his initial communication of words, paint on paper, or loud chords on the piano. However, once the words are heard, the paint on paper or the chords have resounded, the original expression is communicated into objectification. In other words, it has been recorded outside of the originator and can be heard or seen by someone else. There is usually a judgmental response on the part of the communicator as well as the chance that those in whose direction the communication is turned may accept it as having been communicated to them. If they choose to respond, there is interaction.

Thus a communication may be self-interactive, as when I react in a judgmental way to my own feeling as expressed in blobs of paint, or it may be socially interactive as when you say, "I do not like your painting."

LANGUAGE ARTS MEDIA

Language arts media are those methods of expression which utilize verbalisms of one sort or another. Mary tells a story; Peter role-plays the part of a king; Jerry sings a song; little Jon chants, "chug, chug, chug" as he pushes a boat about the floor, while his big sister writes a treatise on nest-building activities of the spider. Words, in some form, are used to communicate in some way. The word *arts* implies that there are ways of doing this, acceptable, experimental, etc. Language arts often may be encouraged and developed from other less clarified and more spontaneous forms of communication, particularly nonverbal communication.

Nonverbal and Verbal Communication

Communication, both nonverbal and verbal, is an important, even necessary, part of each self as it turns outward and tests itself in the world outside. Response results in interchange. Through interaction, the self-image is created and shaped as the child asserts himself and receives positive or negative reactions to his explorations. When healthiest, a positive self-image is original, individual, and unique.

Though the child must accept society, as indeed he is accepted, this does not mean subordination, complacency, or acquiesence of the self. The relationship of the self and society should be a mutually interactive one. Creative communication is an exciting part of such interaction in the developing of one's own life sphere.

Nonverbal communication is a part of this development of each one of us. Creativity is its means and end. For instance, the bodily movement in free rhythmic dance is primarily an act of feeling, which is creating in its very functioning; and yet the completed dance is merely the act begun and ended within temporal and spatial limits. When repeated, and stamped as the creator's own, it may be judged objectively and considered a product or end. Thus thought interacts with what feeling has brought forth. While sensations and ideas, feelings and thoughts, can never be entirely separated, the creative act in its origin tends to be couched primarily in the context of feeling. Although thought takes place, what one hears or sees is first responded to in terms of feeling. The first effort to be creative on the child's part should not be a thoughtful exercise. If it is, it loses its spontaneity and originality. The nursery school child who hesitates to express just what the music is saying to *him* is very open to imitation. It is always easier to follow. When a young child chooses what to emulate, the adult standard usually takes over. The child thinks, "What do they want?" Then he endeavors to give what "they" want, which is easily done. Preferably creativity should function as an outgrowth of feeling in its initial expression. Once objectified as an expression, ideas and thoughts interact with sensation and feelings in the created form and pattern. As contrasted with the taught dance, the imitated picture, and the copied sculpture, which all require observation and thought, the creative act originates in feeling. However, thinking and feeling are soon intermingled. Futher renditions tend to couple the two in the repeated act. Creative writing is one such repeated creative act. In a discussion of this matter, Blanche Jefferson states that

> Creative expression helps each student to face his own thoughts and feelings. . . . We do not always face what our own feelings really are. . . . We try to hide our real feelings . . . They [children] care so deeply about what their parents, teachers, friends think of them that they try to conform to what they are expected to do or feel . . . The teacher needs to help the child focus upon what his real feelings are and to help him identify them.[5]

---

[5]Blanche Jefferson, *Teaching Art to Children* (Boston: Allyn and Bacon, Inc., 1959, 1969), pp. 27-28.

While this is basic, it is necessary that the feeling is objective enough to have achieved expression before it is identified and accepted. Sometimes considerable adult support is necessary when the expression is negative. The cultural "ought" implied earlier is stated by Jefferson's "they try to conform to what they are expected to do and feel." All too often the cultural "ought" acts as a censor before the expression takes place. Thus feelings are crippled and the expression is not genuinely creative. In fact, it may lack most of the characteristics of genuine expression and become mere mechanical or semimechanical movement with body, crayon, or brush. The expression or product becomes a meagerly made imitation of what some one else has done. While imitation may have a place, it should not be used as imposed restrictive authority. Instead, it is a source of possibility to the child, which functions at a later stage as *one* source when he struggles to add ways to the possible solution of how to present his interpretation. Used as additional data in solving the problem of just how to polish initial expression of feeling, it may hold a valuable place. For instance, John has drawn his dog with great enthusiasm. Once objectified, the picture does not quite resemble his dog. John struggles to make his feeling, which has been objectified in the sketch, and his thought coincide. At this point a picture showing how the ears are, for example, may be very useful. This is a piece of data and differs from a dog picture as a model to be imitated. This, too, is very different from offering a child your pattern as a model for him to copy. The latter, since it is *your* model, adds unnecessary emotional complications.

Verbal communication uses numerous media. The baby chants, "Da da da," and taps with his spoon as he sits in his chair; he recites a rhyme in the pre-kindergarten; he sings in the second grade. Language sounds are communicated through the rhythm of his "Da da da" and singing. Chanting, which accompanied his tapping, changed from sounds to syllables and then to words. The voice speaks in monologue, dialogue, and choral form. The child writes and directs the pen in prose which becomes a story, captions, or directions. Chants become songs, rhymes, verse, or poetry. Singing combines sound and word, as does reading. He participates in group planning, regular play, or dramatic play and combines voice with motion and materials. Role playing—whether in open-ended situations, socio- or psychodrama—as well as chanting and rhyming uses the medium of modified voice. Puppets necessitate figures to accompany the voice, thus combining media. And so the list grows and could be continued. When the child uses materials to communicate, the expression tends to be as forceful, or more forceful than pure sound or motion; but the message is less direct in terms of the communicator.

Relationships Between Media

The numerous interrelationships among the various language media are rather obvious. For instance, Alan, a first grader, learns the word *house* as a sight word. Having previously learned *mother* as well as many of the initial consonant sounds, he is able to read a new word, *mouse,* and says, "The mouse ran into the house." Later, he is heard to say, completely of his own volition, while drawing a picture of a mouse,

> *The mouse, the mouse,*
> *Ran into the house,*
> *My little white mouse.*

The alert teacher writes this down, and later reads Alan's rhyme to the class. Thus voice, reading, drawing, and creative verse making were all interrelated during a first grader's morning. After the teacher gave him a manuscript copy of his rhyme, Alan wrote it in his own booklet and thus added another form of communication. If the same kind of experience had happened in third grade, Alan would have written down his own rhyme, and thus would have added to the class collection of creative writing.

Another example further illustrates the interrelationships between media. The sixth graders were complaining about parental demands that they retire early on school nights. The problem situation, as the teacher saw it, was two-fold: going to bed was the obvious external cause. However, the problem in the larger, deeper sense was resistance to parental authority. In order to clarify the problem and to reach one or more solutions, she set up a role-playing session, immediately after reading an improvised dialogue between Mrs. James and Bobbie. Several alternative endings were played out, and the most plausible replayed until numerous possibilities had been exhausted. Consensus about a tentative solution was reached and the children were to test it that night by requesting that they retire five minutes earlier and be permitted to read in bed for exactly twenty minutes. During the course of role playing, this tentative solution of the larger problem, too, was recognized. One girl said, "Gee, I haven't talked to my parents like this for ages." Later, three wrote up their problem in play form, two together and one by herself, as

"Our Problem About Bed Time." Both the immediate problem of going to bed and the problem of resistance had had attention. Ways to the solution of the problem of resistance received further attention, as children began to clarify their relationships to their parents. The teacher and class acted as critics and assisted in sharpening up and polishing the dialogue, both written and during the role-playing sessions. The two final results were group creative writing products. These received further polishing after the members of the class had tried out their agreed-upon plan.

Only one other example of combining communication media need be mentioned here. Two first graders drew pictures of people and cut them out. Inasmuch as they began to utilize them as puppets, the teacher brought out oak tag and elastics. In about five minutes they had simple hand puppets and, without wasting a minute, squatted down behind a table and immediately began an argument about the relative merits of two local ball teams. Later, two other children made oak tag hand puppets and joined as audience. At this point, the teacher took down one of these situations on a cassette and played it back. Later, she wrote it out; before two weeks had passed, most of the class could read it themselves. Had the children been older, they could have written this out themselves. The teacher's function as a recorder is important before children are adept at writing. The teacher, at this time, is merely an intermediary between the child's expression and the recording of it. For expression, written or otherwise, to be creative, it must be the child's own. The adult who acts as recorder must refrain from corrections.

THE TEACHER AS
RECEPTOR AND GUIDE

For creative writing to flourish, it is especially important that the teacher be a receptor rather than a direct giver, and a guide rather than a dictator. The distinctions have certain differences in terms of approach, mood, and result.

The receptor receives the child's contribution openly and cheerfully. Such a teacher is accepting of the child's creative efforts. While he may need all sorts of help in order to express himself clearly and in correct English, the receptive teacher knows that when she is given a piece of creative writing by the child, it is neither the time to teach grammar nor to chastise him for misspelled words. Her approach to the entire situation is encouraging and receptive to what is offered.

Encouragement and acceptance help to establish a relaxed mood, an atmosphere conducive to creative writing. A mood without tension fosters more creativity than a tense one because a relaxed state of being is conducive to the free-flowing expression of feeling. The flowing of feeling is part of the process of writing creatively. The process should be objectification of the free flowing of the child's own feeling. Once this has taken place initially, the child is on his way. He is engaged in the process of creative writing.

While there are numerous times when a more experienced writer may function at an optimum level while under a state of tension, this does not usually apply to the initial stages of children's creative writing. Until they become more seasoned, and frequently even then, the flow of creative expression in written form pours forth more freely in a relaxed situation. Tension at such a time is likely to result in the quickest way to resolution, perhaps complete withdrawl or imitation. Needless to say, neither of these is desired.

The process and its character are reflected in the end result or product. By utilizing the procedure of encouragement and acceptance, the teacher as receptor has a product that is really the child's own. Inasmuch as there was no intimidation, what the child has written shows certain creative characteristics. It is his own.

The teacher as guide rather than dictator has set up an approach which is free and easy as well as encouraging to the child. If the teacher does not present his own patterns to copy either from the chalkboard or from what is said, and if he establishes himself as a kind of resource center, the child knows that he may request help and that it will fit in with what he has chosen. At times, too, when he can't seem to move ahead, the teacher is there to guide him so that he has tools, ideas, or resources from which to draw. The teacher as a center for possible help, as a stimulus to the heretofore untried, and as one who does not overwhelm the child can be conducive to furthering the child's creative work.

It is almost unnecessary to point out the importance of close rapport between teacher and child. A functioning give-and-take relationship makes it easier for each child to seek the help that he finds he requires just when he needs it. Such a relationship makes it easier, too, for each child to share an unfinished piece, to confide his feelings which may be surprising even to him, and to be negative or even hostile when he genuinely needs to be.

The teacher as a guide moves the child ahead when he is ready and thus prevents fruitless plateaus. At the same time, she is catalyst enough to prevent a static situation. If something is needed to build up a sagging situation, the teacher knows how to add it. The very atmosphere should bespeak a creative mood.

The teacher as guide knows each individual and values him as a self for what he does. By not establishing herself as a model, such a teacher develops the child's self-image to see himself for what he is and can do, and not as a blind follower or emulator. The results show individuality and in themselves frequently indicate new developments in the child. After all, one of the roles of any teacher is to foster development. What more important function is there than to actualize the creative potentiality in each child!

The Heron Stood on One Leg

Constance McCullough says "all writing that comes out of the head and heart of the child instead out of the book or out of the teacher's mouth may be said to be creative writing."[6] However, what happens next? Should punctuation be taught? What about long structureless sentences?

The child is a part of society, and there are standards for written work. What of these? Too many teachers take a path designed to please convention and, hopefully, to assist John in attaining acceptability. Eventually, convention does have to be considered. However, perpetuation through imitation is not what is meant. Isn't individuality some sort of a convention? Shouldn't it be? While "The hurun stode on won legg" may not be the quintessence of creative writing, it does express John's creativity. Of course, one can openly chastise John for his spelling and thereby prevent his further adventures in creativity. It might be ignored, but then he does need to spell and to understand the distinction between *won* and *one,* and to spell them correctly for simple objective items, also. The wise teacher knows how to correct the heron while preserving John's creativity.

Miss Stiles notes that (a) during the past three days, ten children have misspelled *one.* She sees that (b) four have misspelled *stood,* but that (c) John alone has used and misspelled *heron.* As to *legg,* she believes that further work with doubling consonants after the short vowel sound and before adding *ing* will take care of that. As a result of her findings, Miss Stiles seeks to correct each of the first three items in a different way.

(a) During the past three days, not only have ten children misspelled *one* when they meant it as a number, but other words from

---

[6]Constance McCullough, *Handbook for Teaching the Language Arts* (San Francisco: Chandler Publishing Company, 1969), p. 53.

other children's work were frequently incorrect. From the total collection, Miss Stiles compiled a list of words for class study. She explained how the list was derived.

(b) *Stood* is a more difficult word. During an interval, Miss Stiles collected the four children who had used the word and misspelled it. She wrote it on the board, had them say it together, spell it together, shut their eyes and spell it again, and then put it in their individual notebooks under "Special Words."

(c) John was the only one who had used and had misspelled *heron*. He wrote it into his notebook under "My Words." He was encouraged to learn to spell it and, during the following week, was asked casually by the teacher whether he could write it on the chalk board.

Legg was treated as part of a larger class learning experience in connection with doubling consonants before endings.

Thus Miss Stiles treated each child's misspelling in terms of his own and his class's needs. It would have been foolish, in her estimation, to have everyone work at a word spelled correctly by most of the children. At the same time, Miss Stiles could see no reason for everyone to learn, at that time, to spell *heron*.

Grammatical difficulties and punctuation errors were treated in the same way that the misspelled words were. Her assessment of whole group, small group, and individual needs as well as a knowledge of general curricular expectations for her grade caused Miss Stiles to utilize what she considered "the right moment." When interest is high, effort is greater. John wanted to make his heron story clear and correct enough to be read by anyone. This came later after his initial writing of it. Feeling was uppermost as he wrote it down for the first time. His judgment came into play with his feelings, after it became objictified on paper.

Miss Stiles recognized the importance of source and self. The self creating should not be hampered until what is to be said is written. The source of creative writing can be snuffed out with hindrances about technical matters. The self creating and communicating utilizes what it already has as tools, but the expression of feeling pours from a deep source of experience within and wants no grammar lesson while it is being caught and put down. Later, yes, but not while the writing is being done. If the child asks for a word or other help, fine! Give it quietly and quickly so as not to break into his thread of continuity. This is not the time to say "Why Ellen, we learned that last week." Ellen is communicating from deep within herself. Catching her up, causing other emotions to come in—such as guilt because "I should have known"—tends to destroy what the child is trying to do at this time. Actually, Ellen will note many of her own errors later when she looks at her product and assesses it critically.

Thus the teacher is always a receptor, but her guiding functions vary in terms of her knowledge of each child and the particular stage of the creative writing process in which he is.

General Expectations

Neither the setting up of absolute and specific objectives on the one hand nor complete laissez-faire activity on the other is recommended. However, it is feasible to hold some general expectations for the creativity of each child. Specifics are developed in terms of the particular child in his particular context. Thus considerable flexibility is fostered. At the same time there are foci for the activities through which each is functioning.

Although young children cannot verbalize their expectations, the adults concerned about them can and do express general expectations for each child as well as for the class as a whole. During the year each child, through what he does, adds the particulars. Stated briefly, each child has the right to expect the following:

1. The development of personal expression through at least one form of creative writing
   Inasmuch as each child is different, his own writing is not like that of anyone else. Each should have opportunities to develop most fully the particular form of creative writing which seems most peculiar to himself at the same time that he attains a general awareness of other types. Thus in the fifth grade Mary may write lovely Haiku while Peter creates blood-and-thunder tales. Each becomes aware of the possibilities possessed by the other.

2. The ability to function through at least one form of nonverbal communication
   Nonverbal communication, as we shall see, frequently precedes or accompanies verbal communication. Richness of the former appears to have a positive effect on the latter. Thus each child should have access to nonverbal forms of communication.

3. The development of a functioning interrelationship between some nonverbal and some verbal forms of communication
   One form of communication enriches rather than precludes another form; nonverbal and verbal forms should flow freely

back and forth in a reciprocal relationship. For instance, the child who claps together two blocks in rhythm and who then expresses a chant-song in the same rhythm expresses such an interrelationship.

4. The encouragement of his own means of creativity as one means of realization
   Each child can and should express his own feelings outwardly. Such outward expression of feeling is one means to self-realization. The myriad forms of creativity and the feelings from which they originate, providing they assume no harmful outward expression, should be encouraged.

5. The exposure to a constant variety of experiences
   Everyone has active periods of doing and reflective periods of undergoing the reactions and results of such activity. These are the two aspects of experience. Creativity springs from the feelings nourished by experience.

6. The recognition of his personal feeling as a potential force in creativity
   Personal feelings are the underlying initiators of genuine creativity. When strong, they stir to the surface in creative expressions.

7. The fostering of the feeling–thinking liaison
   Once the feeling rises to the surface, it may be caught in some form of expression. Objectification in any form is something which can be judged. Thinking and feeling merge, and during this stage the former can and should become dominant at certain times. The final form assumed by the objectified feeling is dependent upon the combined feeling–thinking process.

8. The acceptance of his creative efforts
   The accepting teacher gives the child unlimited security and encouragement. The "first" poem will be written and submitted to the accepting teacher. Otherwise it may never be removed from the bureau drawer. A mite of acceptance may do wonders for some child's potentialities.

9. The fostering and guarding of his uniqueness against acquiescence to imitation
   The dominating teacher achieves an acquiescent classroom. Instead, differences need to be fostered. Each child's right to vary from his peers needs to be maintained even though each is part of a group.

10. The freedom granted to express his feelings so long as they increase his realization and do not deter that of others
    Self-realization is one part of the *summum bonum.* However, it is less than nothing without social-realization. Self and society must be in equilibrium. Social-self-realization is to be sought in terms of the rights and obligations of each child and of each group.

11. The encouragement of the creative writing process through which each communicates outwardly
    Children thrive on encouragement. Initial cautious attempts require careful nurturing.

12. The protection from the kind of criticism and correction of creative writing which tends to stem its flow
    Positive criticism at the proper time develops the creative writer, while devastating critical remarks may stem the flow of the creativity that could have been.

13. Correction in positive ways which meets his individual needs and those of society
    The general expectation of the social-cultural context and self-needs are interrelated. Both aspects as well as the two in reciprocal relationship may need positive suggestions, criticisms, and changes. The responsible adult will make these in ways to foster realization.

14. Encouragement to appreciate the efforts of others even though they differ greatly from his own
    Appreciation of difference is a necessity in today's world; and even were it not, each will develop greater richness of self through being aware of, and responsive to, the differences manifested by those around him.

15. The actualizing of his creative potentiality in ways to develop growth and continuing realization
    A continuous growth process focussed toward realization, rather than the exploitation of the child's immediate gifts, is to be sought for the ultimate realization of the individual.

16. Enjoyment of the satisfaction of having give-and-take with his peers about his creative writing
    Appreciation of the efforts of one's peers in an interactive situation tends to expand the appreciator's view.

17. Being spared the uselessness of license being mistaken for freedom

Freedom for the opportunity to create responsibly and freedom from narrow restrictions tend to foster self-discipline, a
necessity to genuine creative writing.

18. Being led to think reflectively in order to try to solve the prob-
    lems of how better to express what he has said
    Once feeling is objectified into words, the problems of refor-
    mulation necessitate use of the problem-solving, or reflective,
    method of thinking.

19. Gaining the ability to judge the product of his creativity reflec-
    tively
    Being objective about what was subjective requires maturity
    and a positive self-acceptance. The understanding adult real-
    izes that an interval is frequently necessary between the ex-
    pression of feeling in words and a thoughtful evaluation.

20. Finding genuine realization through some form of creative
    writing
    Although everyone cannot become a gifted writer, the foster-
    ing of whatever creativity each child possesses is a resource
    which he should have for the present and the future.

Thus it should be clear that creative writing has a context from
which it comes and by which it develops. The teacher plays an
important twin role: first, negatively, not to stifle creative expression
through autocratically presented models or controls; second, posi-
tively, to be positive and accepting while being aware of when to
offer help and of the ways best to do this in order to maintain the
child's own developing individual creativity. While these are general
expectations, individual children put in the specifics. Some of the
illustrations in the chapters to follow will indicate more fully what
these are. There will be recommendations, too, of procedures which
have been found to be useful and worthwhile. You are urged to
continue to add your own. Creative writing *does* need nurturing.

2

They "Bursted into Jam"

*Some preschool precursors to creative
writing; how and why communicating
through various nonverbal and verbal
media precedes writing creatively.*

Although creative writing, correctly defined, cannot be said to begin
until the child can write, there are precursors which are important
to its development. These can be focused upon by the teacher in the
nursery school, pre-kindergarten, and kindergarten. If she deems
them important enough and utilizes them, she is increasing the ex-
pressiveness of the child. How many of us listen when the young
child speaks? Do we really hear what he says? Can we accurately
repeat his inflections, use of colorful sounds, syllables, and words? If
we listen, and treat the child as though what he was saying was
worthy of our attention, he will be encouraged. Each child has his
own particular way of expression which needs to be fostered.

Creative expression begins as whole body movement which is
refined as the child matures. As particular movements become more
differentiated, certain children express themselves more fully in one
type than in another. They are more creative, for example, through
the use of their legs in dancing than in throwing a ball. Mary creates
through dance expression and Alan through the way he beats his
drum. Alex creates through clay and Ann through the use of finger
paint. However, these activities are interrelated; and all stem originally from feeling which wells up from within the child. Other refine-

21

ments develop as the child matures in the particular kind of expression in which he is most proficient. Other media are used with varying degrees of creativity.

The beginnings of creative writing develop from early verbal communication. However, this verbalism develops from bodily movement, the use of art media, dramatic play, the verbalization of early chants, as well as from the accounts, stories, and songs which the child relates and which he hears. The child communicates creatively through these spontaneous means long before he writes creatively.

PRESCHOOL VERBAL COMMUNICATION[1]

Robert, age four, paused for breath. As he threw out his arms, he said, "And that kitten got fatter and fatter until she burst. She bursted into jam." With a smile of satisfaction, Robert stopped. "That's my story," he said. At four, when children have a fluent command of English and feel secure in the preschool situation, such accounts are likely to pour forth rather easily.

Arthur, also four, stated clearly and confidently, "One day my Dad and me built a great big city. It was bigger than a whale. It had houses in it and, do you know what we did? We made an airport on top of the city. We made a chute to go to it." While the whale was strictly Arthur's, the rest was clear reporting.

The bilingual or non-English-speaking child, in contrast, points to her new dress and says, "Tessa new dress. Tessa like red." Another, with a more imaginative turn, spreads her arms and twirls as she says, "Tina new dress. Tina like. Tina dance and dance. Tina lovely lady."

Three year olds, as a group, tend to be far less facile than four year olds in terms of vocabulary, phrase, and sentence structure. Their factual or imaginative expression, of course, tends to be more limited. Single words and short phrases, accompanied by gestures, are more typical of the young three year old.

Patsy is holding her doll close to her. As she pats its head, she says, "Dolly sick today. Poor dolly." The little boy pushing a truck across the nursery floor is likely to chant "chug, chug" or "garumph, garumph." This may be repeated over and over until at some point he

---

[1]I have collected and remembered children's expressions throughout a long teaching career. Most of the "expressions" in this chapter are adapted from those of children at the Midtown Ethical Culture School. A few are from statements by children at Hudson Guild, the Campus School at New York State University College for Teachers at Buffalo, and a few from observation at inner-city schools in Brooklyn, New York.

embellishes the ending with "Crash bang," and causes the truck to collide with a table leg. At times the identities of boy and truck seem meshed into one. At other times the child controls the truck. Ronny was identified with his truck through the "garumph" and then asserted his individual identity as *he* caused the crash.

By age five, factual information can be stated with an underscoring of the importance of the event and/or the verbalization of a newly acquired phrase. Nina, just turned five, well illustrates this: "I went out yesterday in my *nice new* Easter suit. Daddy took pictures of me and Ned in our *nice new* clothes. We went to see Uncle Henry and we saw his cat." At this particular time, the "nice new clothes" were of more importance than the cat.

The communication of three, four, and five year olds tends to stress what is important to the child at the time. A certain drum beat is repeated over and over. The "daddy" is taller than his house. When shoes become important at age five or so, they are large and may include certain details such as bows, high heels, or buckles, although the other parts of "my mother" may be very simple and rather underdeveloped. In the verbal communications above, "Dolly," "Tina," and "the nice new clothes" are central. The statements of children of these ages are usually very direct with no unnecessary preliminaries.

These communications were recorded as follows: during the work and play period in the cases of Tessa, Tina, Patsy, and Ronny; during the time the group had gathered near the piano for stories and music in the instances of Robert, Arthur, and Nina. During the work and play period the teacher noted them down, responded cheerfully to Tessa and Tina, and said nothing then to Patsy and Ronny. When the group was all assembled together for a few minutes, Patsy was asked, "How is your dolly today?"

The response might be similar to the one above which had been heard earlier. On the other hand, the attention span of the three year old and the lapse of time might well cause the little girl to state her feelings about this as a new experience unrelated to the preceding one. Thus she could answer almost anything. If Ronny, also three, were asked two hours later whether he could make a sound like his truck and if the truck were held up, he might well repeat the same sound. Again, he might not because this is another feeling reaction which has had one more intervening experience—namely the earlier one—on which to build. Three year olds have short interest spans. For this reason, the teacher should record, on the spot, anything she wants to keep as statements from her children.

This points up another problem. Do we want the child to respond in the same way with the same sound to the sight of a truck? The teacher who does will repeat the same sound, be sure that Ronny and his friends repeat it, and thereby habituate the children to it. Then the next time they see it, the conditioned response will be repeated. This is fine, if education is nothing but habit training and conditioning. A small guinea pig can be taught to squeal every time he hears the sound of the refrigerator door, *if* he is fed right after hearing the sound enough times. Are our children guinea pigs? Must they be habituated to everything? Certainly, they are to form certain habits, respond in certain ways to some stimuli around them. But if we want to develop creative children, there are many areas for which we want Johnny's own response because he is Johnny and not Ned. While both John and Ned should eventually know the sounds for *a* and cannot read it as *ee* if they are to be understood, they will not develop individual feelings if habituated responses are always demanded. There is no reason why Ned should respond, at age three, in the same way as John does to the sight of a truck, if we want two individual children.

Robert, Arthur, and Nina all volunteered their stories, as related above, in response to the teacher's query, "Does anyone have a story to tell us?" It would have been wisest to record these stories earlier in the day, during the work-play period, had they stated them then. However, at story time these children would be more likely to respond in a way similar to their earlier stories because they are older. These four and five year olds would be more likely than the three year olds to retain the same basic account and to add a few embellishments with the second telling. In other words, thinking and feeling might be combined in a way to develop the original account which they had stated and remembered.

Nina obviously enjoyed using the new phrase "nice new." This was evident not only from her use of the phrase which she was adding to her vocabulary, but also from the look on her face as she repeated it. In her case, a second telling might well have added "nice new" to the clothes of Daddy and Uncle Henry.

It is important to remember that young children have short spans of attention. Although they do remember, their temporal and spatial dimensions are not those of adults. "Tomorrow I went to the zoo. It was warm there in the summer," is not atypical for a story told in December.

Adult conceptions of time and space are not usually clear until about age six. It is wisest to take down the "story" or description, the first time it is told, as it is told, *if* the recorder's concern is in original creative verbal expression.

COMMUNICATION THROUGH
BODILY MOVEMENTS

The preschool child is still developing overt speech forms. He tends to express himself yet more fully by using his whole body. The disappointed three year old sags and droops visibly or may give violent vent to his frustrations and fairly bristle all over, quite noticeably, saying "Bad boy" as he kicks the rubber doll with his full strength. "Can't go" may be added, as he projects his disappointment onto the doll.

Danny jumped up and down on the rubber doll. He had run across the room and snatched it from the doll carriage. Then he jumped up and down on it, singing, "Gotta wash that Laurie right out of my hair." This was his expression of real hostile feeling. Baby sister was presenting real problems of sibling rivalry. The doll was a safe victim on which to vent his wrath for, of course, he could not jump on Laurie at home. The song was adapted from what he had heard. His feeling was genuine. His aggressive act of jumping on the doll had therapeutic value. While the teacher was not a therapist, she did realize that he was expressing deep feeling and did not stop him then, although she did take steps to meet his needs and to rechannel his feelings. To the skeptic, it must be added that if the doll had been another child, his feelings would have been rechanneled then and there. An important point to be observed was that, although the words said what Danny meant, his hostility was stated in a complete bodily response. Whole body emotional response is frequently still part of adult patterns, although it may be sublimated and sometimes is barely visible.

As the young child gains greater physical maturity and muscular control, he responds more and more with differentiated bodily movements. He rocks, sways or nods, taps his fingers, hops on one foot or tip toes in the rhythmic response he feels as the result of an external stimulus. The rocking of the four year old may be accompanied by chanted syllables such as "Boomba, boomba, boomba." Differentiated bodily movements in a definite pattern represent one type of nonverbal communication.

A stimulus—sound, sight, touch—from without causes the child to respond by making overt signs. When such a sign is a focused motion, such as a wave of greeting to Daddy as he comes down the street and into the visual field of son Jimmy, who is perched inside on the window sill, it is a type of conscious nonverbal communication. The importance of this as a precursor to verbal communication cannot be overstressed. Without digressing into a discussion of nonverbal communication as a source of insight into emotional difficulties, it suffices to say that the young child's nonverbal communication is frequently richer and more genuinely communicative than the verbal communication which develops and follows it.

The young child is able to move his whole body more easily than he is able to make distinctive intricate movements. Many whole body movements are more natural to him than speech. The two or three year old child who does not like what another does is likely to hit first and protest verbally later. By age four, he may hit and shout "No, no." It is still hard for some five year olds to say "no" first. Hitting or pushing another away is more natural in that it is a pattern established more easily than speech and, developmentally, is prior to it. By age eight, however, one expects the child to use language first. Fists are used even then, but not usually until after some verbal encounter has preceded this act of greater overt hostility. However, less overt nonverbal communication is still a part of adult language. The raised eyebrow, the tapping of the foot—with or without music —and specific types of throat scraping are all part of nonverbal communication in the adult world.

The non-English-speaking child, especially, needs a receptive person for his nonverbal communication. Carmen studied herself in the mirror on the dresser in the housekeeping corner, then patted her hair as she smiled. Turning, she smiled at Dora and continued to pat her hair. The teacher smiled and said, "Carmen's hair is pretty." Carmen responded with harder pats and repeated, "Hair pretty."

The little girl who listens to a recording of Tschaikowsky's *The March of the Toys*[2] may respond suddenly with jerky arm movements and do this over and over. If another child questions this with "What you doin?" she may not really know and answer, "Nothin!" Rhythmic communication may not always represent an act or object to be named. It may express feelings of anguish or well-being that are expressions of the child's whole state of being, rather than expressing a specific feeling for a particular thing.

Nonverbal communication at ages three, four, and five is manifested in a variety of ways. As we said above, one of the most common is through bodily movements. In order to encourage, and in a sense, to confirm its importance, the preschool teacher seizes upon some of

---

[2]"The March of the Toys" from *The Nutcracker Suite* by Peter Tschaikowsky, Columbia Record MX 151. (Throughout this book I recommend particular recordings and translations that are especially good for classroom use.)

these movements and gives them musical accompaniment. The raising and lowering of arms develops into the flying of pigeons, if the child so terms it, and the hopping of the four year old becomes a bunny jumping about a garden. However, such "bunny patterns" must arise from the children. The galloping horse, the putt-putting speed boat, or the clat, clatting el train determine the musical accompaniment given. Thus the creative rhythmic expression receives acceptance and confirmation of its pattern. It is designated as being important. The adult must refrain from naming it. Pigeons, rabbits, boats and el trains should develop as verbal descriptions from the child as his movement suggests an experience which he has had and/or with which he can identify. Later, he will state that he wants "bird music."

At age three, the child's movements tend to be rather closely confined to the area immediately adjacent to the spinal axis of the body and thus are restricted in spatial mobility. Muscular coordination is less advanced and controls are maintained with shaky confidence. Large muscular development is proceeding more rapidly than that of the small muscles. As a result of developing coordination, the child is gaining security gradually in his directed movements.

Once control over directed movements is better established, usually at age four or so, his spatial area of mobility increases and the child is, to a considerably greater extent, the conscious director of his bodily movements. As habitual motions require less attention, the child experiments in a variety of ways. As he does so, his nonverbal communication through bodily signs increases in control and variety. At four his newly found muscular skills are not as smoothly executed as they will be at a more mature stage. However, inasmuch as general bodily controls are established enough to permit such basic activities as running, hopping, etc. without special conscious consideration, experimenting with what he can and cannot do goes on constantly. Peter may climb up high on the jungle gym and want to communicate his bravado by jumping off or trying to fly down like a pigeon. All of a sudden, he realizes his inadequacy and retreats. Nonverbal communication through bodily rhythm may reach a high level of grace, control, and beauty, especially in girls. However, the necessary controls are still somewhat erratic and lack of developed coordination is constantly evident. This is especially evident in small muscular movements because the finer controls tend to develop more slowly. More four year olds, however, can skip with one foot, run, gallop, jump, and sway. Such coordinations are helpful in communicating nonverbally, although bodily communication is not confined to these movements alone.

The greater muscular control, extended imagination, and general environmental "know how" join to give most five year olds considerable scope for nonverbal rhythmic communication. Five year olds tend to embellish with greater details the basic controls established at four. For instance, cowboys may ride *after cattle* rather than just gallop as they did at age four; puppies play and *chase kittens* now, birds not only fly as they did at age four, but fly *home to feed their babies in a nest,* or various circus animals and performers come to life clearly enough to be recognized in the five year old's kindergarten. Even the rhythmic beat and grind of the garbage truck is expressed in some detail.

"I feel like a pony today," is expressed rhythmically at four, without a word being said. At age five, ponies step along, gaily pulling carts in a parade. When the "ponies" begin of their own volition, the teacher should accompany them and follow their rhythm. The "ponies" are creations resulting from exuberant feeling and need to be expressed as each child feels it. This is quite antithetical to having the teacher say "Now, we'll all be ponies," which controls the children and implies acquiescence to a teacher-made pattern. One pony is a creative act on the part of the initiator. The other children's ponies may be partly creative and partly imitative. The distinctions here may be a bit difficult. However, they represent a type of creative expression more genuinely based on children's feelings than the ponies set up and initiated by the teacher.

COMMUNICATION THROUGH ART MEDIA

Graphic nonverbal communication is expressed through the use of paint, finger paint, clay, and other media. The manipulation of paint on paper with a tightly clutched brush at first communicates little more than the desire to put the paint on the paper. Developing hand, finger, and hand-eye coordination is evident. The way he feels the paint with hand or finger seems closely related to the child's own feeling. The child expressing a feeling of caution daintily places one finger into the paint while the exuberant, and sometimes the hostile child, tends to plunge both hands right into it. The bright free-moving swirls at age three can communicate the delight and freedom from tension of the child painting them. Pounding and poking at a lump of clay indicates the child's state of emotional feeling as well as initial use of an art medium.

Given plenty of experience, the manipulation stage, related to a child's general feeling state, usually has developed into the symbolic stage by age four or so. What was painted in a generally happy mood suggests something which is stated proudly. "These are the roads in the Adirondacks," or pointing to a streak above some clustered swirls and solids, "That's the El over the cars by the project." Rather quickly, this stage develops into the painting of the realistic type of picture. At this stage, the child decides ahead of time what he will do. His feelings are expressed to himself, sometimes overtly, too, and his statement, "I am going to paint my house," precedes the application of paint to paper.

"This is my house. My father is in it. You can't see him" or "This is a big fence. Men are by it" are the "stories" told about the pictures. While there is no need here to digress about the numerous intermediary points between the manipulative, symbolic, and the realistic stages, it should be stated that keeping colors separated, making stripes and spots are all evidences of the child's clarifications to himself of how he feels and of what he is doing. The child tends to develop similarly in his use of all art media providing he develops at his own pace and with occasional guidance rather than adult prescriptions.

The child's statements made spontaneously about his work should be recorded neatly under the pictures or on paper near his clay work. Careful manuscript at the bottom, or in an unpainted corner, records exactly what was said. Imaginative combinations of reality and fantasy as well as the pure fact are frequent. The words told to the teacher are part of the child's creative act. Since he cannot yet write them, Jimmy's verbal expressions must be recorded for him. However, Jimmy must not be questioned specifically. His own spontaneous expression is what is sought, *not* his response to what he thinks the adults want to hear.

"Will you tell us about your picture?" may be used because it leaves Jimmy free to answer what he wishes or to refuse. It implies no prescription and leaves him free to refuse. "What is that?" or "Is that a dog?" quickly transmit to him the impression that it must be something and that he has to be ready to state what it is. This restricts his spontaneity and tends to channel his verbalizations. Later, Jimmy will write it out for himself. The respect given him early, the fact that what he said warrants recording, and the pleasure in the give and take about the picture or other art work with the adult, and perhaps with his peers, all nourish the growth of creativity.

It may be noted, too, that the child frequently pounds or pokes clay in rhythm, that he may paint while music is playing, and that spontaneous verbalizations may accompany what he is doing. Sometimes play with syllables is heard. At other times, "Piff, piff, poof, pumb, pumb, pumb, pumble, pumb, pumb, pumb, pumble" accompanies his work with clay. "Spot, spot, see me make spots," may be chanted while he paints them.

Thus we find that nonverbal communication through art media may utilize one material or may combine more than one kind of expression. The verbal and nonverbal may also be combined in one act.

Dramatic Play

Dramatic play is a veritable nursery for verbal and nonverbal creativity. The tiny child utilizes objects around him as projections of himself and pets them or spanks them. Slowly, he verbalizes his feelings and gradually personifies imaginative play with objects.

The young three year old reaches out from solitary play, or from processional or side-by-side play, to interactive play with one other child and then with a small group. At the same time his verbalization develops and should be given the fullest possible opportunity to expand. The beginnings of verbalization accompanying his dramatic play of house or bus are the foundations for what he will record later as he writes creatively. Full expression of the little girl's sounds as she quiets her "baby," of the father, who leaves the doll corner "to go to work," or of Tom calling, "Step up, all aboard," as he collects bus tokens, are all familiar to the nursery school teacher.

By age four, verbalization on the part of the English-speaking child has expanded so that coherent accounts can be given through dramatic play of trips, visits, household doings, constructions, etc. The play itself is accompanied by considerable verbalization. At times the correct word is requested and at others, invented, so that the account can continue.

Paul, pushing his bus toward the block garage, shouts, "Out of the way. Coming down Elmwood." Later, as he puts the bus into the structure, "All out, last stop." More or less to himself, he adds, "Now to gas up." To Peter, who is "driving" a car, "Gas up, gas up, and off we go." To the teacher, "What's that thing? Claborator?" "Oh," in response to her correction. Then, "Carburetor. Hey, Pete, my carburetor is stuck." The non-English-speaking child has plenty of chance to add to his vocabulary during this kind of activity. The teacher helps provide words and names of objects. In contrast to Paul, Ramon may say, "Bus, bus," and later, "Bus, bus down street."

The non-English-speaking child needs to be encouraged to continue verbalization. The three year old is likely to speak and to accompany his play with his own native words. By four, though, care must be taken to see that verbalization continues in the native language while it is being replaced by English in the classroom. Too many children have become silent as they become aware of their lack of ability to communicate in English. Feeling insecure and inferior, they cease to communicate in school at all. Better to communicate in any tongue, understood or not understood, than to remain silent. Remaining silent is not natural to the young child. His silence may take months to overcome, if it becomes his pattern during dramatic play.

Dramatic play as an overt behavioral projection may be expressed as reiteration of experience, reconstruction of experience to meet needs and interests, or as imaginative expression. It requires ample time and space for full development. The verbal accompaniment is necessary to maximum growth and to the development, later, of creative writing. By five and six years of age, dramatic play is likely to expand into simple puppetry, more structured role playing, and simple dramatizations which eventually have prepared scripts as children work out their most acceptable presentation of what they are preparing.

From Chants to Stories

The tiny child in his high chair bangs his spoon and says, "Bang, bang." The three year old pushes a wooden boat across the floor and repeats, "Toot, toot, toot" over and over again. By four, this may be embellished and become:

> *Toot, toot, toot, see I'm going,*
> *Toot, toot, toot, see I'm going.*

This is likely to be a chant repeated over and over, often utilizing the major scale. In the housekeeping corner, the baby is frequently put to sleep with a chant:

> *Sleep, sleep, go to sleep,*
> *Sleep, sleep, go to sleep.*

The dishes are placed on the table:

> *One for Daddy, and one for me*
> *One for Daddy, and one for me.*

Chants are a definite aspect of the preschool child's communication and verbalization patterns.

The alert teacher records these simple chants by jotting them down or catching them on a tape recorder. She can develop them from chants sung by one child into group chants or into simple songs. For instance, the boat chant:

Toot, toot, toot, see I'm going

which is repeated can be sung by the teacher and child. Another child may add an ending:

Out to sea, out to sea

Some of the chanted accounts accompanying block construction or housekeeping play may be read to the children as recorded and occasionally reread as stories. For instance, Charlie's

> *Bang, bang, I'm making a house,*
> *I'm making a house,*
> *Bang, bang, nearly made.*

could be a story read to the group. Also, it could be sung using his basic rhythm and a major scale.

It is interesting to note that the chants may be original such as

> *Bang, bang, bang,*
> *Goes my hammer as I'm nailing.*

Frequently these chants employ onomatopoetic sounds and syllables:

> *Boosh, boosh, boosh,*
> *I walked through the puddle.*

They may be:

> *Toot, toot, toot I'm moving.*
> *I'm moving to the sea.*

which is a combination of what has been heard in Lucy Sprague
Mitchell's "Fog Boat Story"[3] and the embellishment of the child's
own ending. Children's chants may be familiar songs chanted, rather
than sung, using the child's own ending:

> *Horses galloping, galloping, galloping*
> *Horses galloping, galloping, galloping*
> *All the way to my house in the country.*

The chants can be imitations, too, of songs heard converted to the
rhythms or sound of the activity itself: "Clang, clang, clang going to
the fire" or "The wheels on the bus go round and round" chanted
rather than sung as the child spins the truck wheels. Chants may be
descriptive:

> *See me, see me*
> *I'm swinging, swinging.*

Or narratives chanted:

> *Rose, Rose was the hippo*
> *We saw her in the zoo,*
> *She slept and slept*
> *Her nose is red and rosy.*

They can also, at age four and five, be imaginative:

> *In my house, I have a tiger*
> *Yes a tiger, yes, a tiger.*
> *In my house my tiger lives and eats with me, eats with me.*
> *He wears a crown and a bright red belt.*
> *My tiger, my tiger.*

Thus the varied lingual expressions, which may be recorded by
hand or on tape, can be developed as songs or stories. They may be
primarily sounds chanted; they may be descriptive, narrative, or
imaginary. As was said above, they may be original, imitative, or
combinations. Whatever their form, the chant is a direct antecedent

---

[3]Lucy Sprague Mitchell, *Here and Now Story Book* (New York: E.P. Dutton & Co.,
Inc., 1921). See especially "The Fog Boat Story."

of later creative verbal expression which the older child will write down himself.

The Place of Books, Stories, and Songs

In the preceding section, spontaneity of expression was emphasized. Unless he is obviously playing with sounds, syllables, or words, and sometimes then, the child expresses something—an experience, a feeling, a thought, a fact, or some combination. His constantly enlarging experiences feed his accounts, stimulate his imagination, develop his expressions of what he feels, and lead him ever further to new and richer expressions.

Books stimulate expression as well as adding vicarious experiences. The child identifies and feels with the characters. They add to the knowledge the child has, and may help him to form patterns for his own expression. It is important that they be accessible, readily handled, and of the types appropriate to the children's age levels, needs, and interests.

Most of us have seen a three, four, or five year old thumb excitedly through a picture book. Clear, bright pictures, with which he can identify readily, presented in an uncluttered, interesting manner in a book which is easy to handle serve as stimuli to verbal expression.

> *See that boy* (pointing).
> *He's big like my brother.*
> *He's sailing a boat.*

as well as

> *Its all over snow.*
> *See it.*
> *Snow can come over you in a snow pile.*

are typical responses to pictures as they are observed by the four, four and a half, and five year old. Later, the four year old remembers, imagines, combines, creates:

> *Boy, boy, sailing, sailing,*
> *Until the snow snowed me all up.*

Loud laughter indicated Mickey's delight with his creation.

The "here and now" experiential story leads to creations with which he associates.

> *That's my park.*
> *My park has hundreds of dogs—big like that.*
> *In my park you can eat ice cream under a tree.*

was stated, as the child built with blocks after hearing *The Park Book.*[4]

The simple, acceptable folk tale, real or imitation, adds rhythm and possible rhyme to what is told later. After hearing *Millions of Cats*[5], which had been read before, Alex said,

> *My fishes cover the wall. There are hundreds, and billions, and billions, and billions of them. One day they ate each other all up. They ate each other up. One didn't. He hid from the fighting. He hid and hid while the others fighted. Bang, bang, bang, they went. Hundreds, and millions, and billions of the fish fighted, [ex]cited, fighted. One didn't. He was Mufty Tufty. Mufty Tufty sat and waited.*

The cumulative type of tale almost invites the child to participate. *Ask Mr. Bear,*[6] a modern tale patterned on the cumulative folk tale, appeals to the child's desire to participate. Psychologically it is far more acceptable than *The Old Woman and the Pig.*[7]

The repetitive parts involve the children, and later, individuals may be heard repeating parts in rhythm. Sometimes these are embellished by the child:

> *And the rabbit ran,*
> *And his mother ran,*[8]
> *And her twin children ran . . .*

This was Tony's addition to the little wild rabbit's run.

The purely imaginative story, when used, may extend the child's own imagination. Mary, carrying a small spade over her shoulder, strode across the playground stating loudly,

> *I'm going to dig up a gooseberry bush and find Peter Rabbit. He'll sleep in my bed with me after his mother don't give him his supper.*

---

[4]Charlotte Zolotow, *The Park Book* (New York: Harper and Brothers, 1944).
[5]Wanda Gag, *Millions of Cats* (New York: Coward-McCann, Inc., 1928).
[6]Marjorie Flack, *Ask Mr. Bear* (New York: The Macmillan Company, 1932).
[7] *The Old Woman and the Pig.* See, for instance, Paul Galdone edition (New York: McGraw-Hill Book Company, 1960).
[8]"The Rabbit Who Was Afraid," in Carolyn Sherwin Bailey (ed.), *Once Upon a Time Animal Stories* (Springfield, Mass.: Milton Bradley Company, 1920).

She had heard *Peter Rabbit*[9] during the preceding day.
Some children repeat words and phrases over and over, such as:

> *Tsk, tsk, tsk.*[10]
>
> *Hundreds and millions and trillions.*[11]
>
> *Pokey, pokey, pokey.*[12]

Children frequently "read" books. They sit and thumb through, stating the part of the story under each illustration correctly. This stimulates their own recollections and adds to the child's knowledge as well as providing additional vocabulary for use.

The stories, rhymes, and verse told may be classified into the same types as books, i.e., "here and now" experiential, simple acceptable folk tales (genuine or imitation), cumulative tales, and purely imaginative stories. However, in addition to enlarging experience, adding to information, imagination, and vocabulary, and encouraging vocabulary development as books do, stories, rhymes, and verse told to the children serve another important function. The teacher telling *Caps for Sale,*[13] *Lambikin,*[14] *Spot the Cat,*[15] or reciting *Mrs. Grump Grundy*[16] knows that she will be joined by her audience at the first or second point of repetition. All the four year olds "sniff, sniff" with Spot's little pink nose and "purr and purr as she curls up warm into a ball of fur."[17] The phrases, words, and sounds come out later during dramatic play and are incorporated into their own stories and accounts. As we have said, imitating, combining, and inventing result from stories. Usually rapport with the teller of the story or verse is much closer than with the reader of a story; certainly, than with the voice on a record. In fact, storyteller and Spot may seem to be almost one. And, in some cases, if Spot is not hurried to the third home where he finds acceptance, the especially sensitive child may sit there with tears rolling down his or her face. This kind of identity of

---

[9]Beatrix Potter, *The Tale of Peter Rabbit* (London: Frederick Warne & Co., Ltd., n.d.).

[10]Esphyr Slobodkina, *Caps for Sale* (New York: William R. Scott, Inc., 1947).

[11]Gag, *Millions of Cats.*

[12]Janette S. Lourey, "The Pokey Little Puppy" in *A Treasury of Little Golden Books* (New York: Golden Press, 1960), pp. 9–13.

[13]Slobodkina, *Caps for Sale.*

[14]"The Story of Lambikin," in Bailey, *Once Upon a Time Animal Stories.*

[15]"How Spot Found a Home," in Mitchell, *Here and Now Story Book.*

[16]James Tippett, "Mrs. Grump Grundy," in *I Live in a City* (New York: Harper and Brothers, 1927).

[17]Mitchell, "How Spot Found a Home."

feeling gives the child an added wealth of experiential and imaginative material with which he is so closely identified that he can express it rather easily. The outgoing verbal child adds these words and expressions to his own story, and may embellish them with his own additions more quickly than the quieter child. This is not to imply that the expression of one is better than the other, merely that it is different.

The story experience, in whole or part, may come forth later as partial expression of a feeling clearly and profoundly felt. For instance, Deena angrily said,

> *And and he putted her out. He put her out, 'Bang,' just like that cross, cross woman putted out Spot.*

Her feeling was definitely Deena's but her verbalization of it drew, in part, from Mitchell.[18]

Songs are added in a similar fashion as well as in context. Introduced in a context of meaning, they may be utilized again by the child in that same context. Later, they find their way into activity in general. For instance, while the preschool child is swinging, the teacher may sing the *Swinging Song*.[19] The next time the child swings, he is likely to find the rhythm of up and down most conducive to repeating, "Swinging, swing-ing" and then finish the song. The teacher, or the child, may introduce this to the group as a whole later on in the day or on another occasion. Two weeks later, Linda is rocking her doll. She "sings" this song to Jean, the doll:

> *Swinging, swing-ing*
> *Now Jean goes up*
> *Swing-ing, swing-ing*
> *Down goes Jean*
> *In her bug-gy*
> *All asleep.*

Linda has combined the rhythm and some of the words with her activities and verbalization of them.

---

[18]Mitchell, "How Spot Found a Home."
[19]"Swinging" in Satis Coleman and Alice Thorn, *Singing Time* (New York: The John Day Company, Inc., 1929), p. 137.

THE TEACHER'S ROLE

The teacher's role may be summarized briefly under eight major functions. These are: being a listener; being interested and encouraging; being ready to record; being able to share; being adept at formulating; being clear about distinctions of origin; being aware of traditional and cultural usages of speech; being ready to incorporate parent cooperation.

Being a Listener

The teacher who wishes to cultivate creative expression must be a fine listener. She listens to what is said to her directly, to what the child states while engaged in an activity, to what he says at other times such as while waiting to go home, while he is looking at a book, or while he sits or rests quietly. She listens to overt expression. As she becomes better acquainted with each child, she notes changes in manner, physical being, attitude, and reactions to materials and to people. These tell her things about the child. What is implied and what is verbalized atune her constantly to keener listening. Overtly, she tries to stop and lend an ear whenever possible. Covertly, she listens for inner signs which the child expresses in a variety of ways and which can be noted by one who is aware.

Being Interested and Encouraging

The teacher is interested when she attends to what the individual child is saying and doing. She is encouraging when she gives moral support and understands. When the child needs some item to realize more fully what he is trying to do, and the teacher provides it, she is supportive and aware of the child's needs and interests. What is needed may be a word:

> *You know, I saw those striped things like horses.*
> *Well, anyway, I saw those . . . those . . .*

Here the teacher should say "zebras." She doesn't make a lesson out of it, or break the child's train of thought. At this juncture, "zebras" is merely the tool necessary to finish what is being said. Similarly, supplementation, rather than outright correction, is preferable because it is important to keep the child's expressions flowing freely. Needless to say, sincere praise is encouraging.

The child, especially the reticent one, almost glows when his statements or accounts are repeated to the group as a whole. If he remembers, he can help to do it himself. If not, the teacher should read what he has said earlier. It gives the child satisfaction when his verbalizations are given status. Also, they may well add to the group's collection of worthwhile accounts. Nothing can be more encouraging than the smile and nod of the interested adult.

Being Ready to Record

A tiny pad and pencil carried in her smock pocket or kept available on top of the piano or cupboard is a must, if the teacher expects to get down accurately just what Susie says when she says it. Of course, a small tape recorder is recommended when it does not interfere, by virtue of its mechanism, or when its use does not divert the child. Children should not always be aware of what is recorded. When they are all telling stories, it may be expected. Otherwise, the less obvious the teacher is, the better. The teacher may wish to read what has been said to the child privately, or to the group, if she deems it of interest. Occasionally, very rhythmic verbalizations may be accompanied with piano, drum, rhythm sticks, or clapping. Recording what is chanted, sung, or said in a class book makes a permanent record. It can be read from readily and may also be a useful item for parent education.

Being Able to Share

Sharing is of tremendous value, socially and emotionally, to each child. "I said it and it was written there by my teacher for all of us to hear" gives ego strength and satisfaction. Sharing is a useful stimulus to others, too, providing it does not lead to imitation. Sharing with other classes personally or by way of the school paper is important, especially if everyone is included. If possible, everyone should be included. Each ego is important; and at this age, each needs recognition. Waiting for the next issue does nothing for the self-image of a five year old.

Being Adept at Formulating and Reformulating

When one child presents a story, chant, or song which seems unfinished, a question or two quietly asked may help the child to finish. The teacher can also read aloud what the child has said. Then she asks the group, "What do you think happened next?" John said,

I went to the country. I saw birds.
I saw birds. Some flew very fast.
I saw birds.

If John is satisfied, fine. The quiet question may be "Did you see what color the birds were?" If John seems more doubtful about additions, the class may be asked whether they have ever seen birds, after the original is reread. They are likely to respond immediately with "I saw . . ." The teacher can then change the story to John and Harry went to the country. She reads that John saw birds and through to the end of what he said and then adds the few lines stating what Harry says he saw.

A chant may end with the last syllable literally dangling on a "fa." The other children are very likely to repeat the end and to bring it down to "do."

Mitchell's books[20] were among the very first to present original child and group expression. Some of the stories received a little editing, refurbishing, or were combinations of what more than one child said. Many teachers have followed this general procedure for years. The rewards in creative expression are many. However, the teacher should hesitate before reformulating. She must be aware, too, of the adult tendency to round off too neatly.

The teacher's role here is, primarily, to encourage each child to express what he feels. The teacher's reformulations do have a place, but too often this is overdone. The children should gain confidence through acceptance of what they have experienced.

Being Clear About Distinctions of Origin

The teacher owes it to her children and parents as well as to other members of the public she serves to be clear about who said what. Words put into the child's mouth, words attributed to one child and said by another, and adult corrections, changes, and "doctoring up" are not to be tolerated. Children's work is not for exhibit as such. Too frequently the work of "genius" has been exploited by an adult who freely refurbished a child's work. Such is not our concern and such acts are to be rejected. Children's expressions honestly recorded or reformulated openly and presented for what they are are all that concern us here.

[20]Mitchell, *Here and Now Story Book* and its successor, *Another Here and Now Story Book* (New York: E. P. Dutton & Co., Inc., 1937).

Being Aware of Traditional and Cultural Uses of Speech

The Jewish child, Chinese child, Black child, Mexican child, and the child of various other ethnic groups all tend to have certain inflections, patterns of word groupage, and pronunciation which are part of their background. Too, the descendent from the Mayflower traveller may have grown up hearing

We'll go when the horses are done eatin'.

Precursors to creative writing need to be original and spontaneous expressions. Calling attention to deviations from accepted usage is not the way to encourage the child to express his thoughts, ideas, descriptions, and rhythmic creations. Repeating what has been said in the accepted manner does let him hear it correctly when done unobstrusively. This is often best done at another time. The teacher needs to remember that her major concern, however, is to be a receptor for what flows forth. At times of creativity one does not correct speech or grammar. Writing down the preceding sentence about the horses is being fair to the child. Later, when it is time to put crayons away, for instance, the teacher can say, "We'll go when you have *finished* cleaning up." The child hears it correctly and clearly. On another occasion, the teacher can ask him for another way to say "done eatin'." This should be during ordinary conversation, not during spontaneously stated exclamations!

Being Ready to Incorporate Parent Cooperation

A parent's meeting on the topic of creativity in young children can be an asset, providing the parents understand English and are interested in furthering creative verbal expression. The teacher must be adamant about the necessity for neither forcing nor exhibiting children. She must be clear about the importance of trying to foster the goals she has for verbal expression. These may be summed up as encouraging creativity verbally, utilizing it as a means of expression as well as a tool toward creative writing later, giving each child the opportunity frequently to feel good about what he says by being able to record and read or sing it back, and above all being encouraging and appreciative of what he says.

In schools with teacher aides or other paraprofessionals, the teacher has a definite advantage. The aide can learn how to record. In the case of non-English-speaking children, the original may be done in Spanish and translated for the rest of the group. Rosita smiled and sat up tall when she heard the teacher read her story in English:

> *We rode in a big, big plane.*
> *We rode and rode.*
> *Water was under it.*
> *Then, in the night, we got off.*
> *Lights were all around.*

The non-English-speaking child does need to learn English. However, his fluency in his native tongue should be recorded as faithfully as that of any one else, when it is possible to do so. When what he says can be shared through translation, he is given an added feeling of belonging to his group which is invaluable to him as an individual whose self-image is developing along with those of everyone else. The child and the class loses out every time a Rosita remains silent!

THEY "BURSTED INTO JAM"

Cats may "burst into jam" in the stories of small boys. Retention by his teacher of spontaneous factual and imaginative expression is something to which each child has a right. Expression through creative writing is a right of the child in the upper grades. In the preschool, he needs to develop, as fully as possible, the kind of expression that he will write later.

3

"Whoopee, I'm a Tree"

*How creating nonsense can lead to
verse writing; some ways to
encourage verse and poetry writing.*

Children like to laugh and do laugh. In the classroom, laughter and fun can be facets of creativity. Feelings of well-being are accompanied by spontaneous sharing. However, there is a distinction between nonsense and silliness, although the point of view from which each is judged partly determines its classification. For instance, while some might define Lear's nonsense[2] as silly, for certain age levels it is accepted as nonsense just because it almost seems to be sensible. In most cases, it deliberately stops just short of silliness and loss of the reader's emotional control and causes laughter. The expected does not occur and the unexpected, while readable, has no serious meaning. The expected is set awry! For example, children at certain age levels only will laugh at a monkey wearing a hat. At age three, the child is not wise and worldly enough to be fully aware that monkeys do not naturally wear hats! Later, having acquired this factual information, the child finds the situation funny. And even later, in the

[1]Grace K. Pratt, "Whoopee, I'm a Tree" in *Elementary English* (October 1966). The first part of this chapter is adapted and enlarged considerably from the magazine article. Used by permission of the National Council of Teachers of English.

[2]Edward Lear, *Nonsense Books* (Boston: Little, Brown, and Company, 1934).

upper grades, the scientific-minded child may remark, "Anyone *knows* that monkeys don't wear hats," while others may remark, "How cute!" To neither is this nonsense that is fun.

All children laugh and react to certain kinds of nonsense. Because nonsense in syllable or word form is often rhythmic, and because rhythm is basic in much creative expression—including verse and poetry—nonsense can lead a child straight to the creation of poetry. Let's find out how one teacher did this.

THE ROLE OF NONSENSE

Meredith, age six, had just become aware of word endings. Throwing out both arms, she shouted, "Whoopee, I'm a tree." This was written on the chalkboard by the first grade teacher, who remarked cheerfully, "Here is Meredith's rhyme. 'Whoopee' and 'tree' sound like each other at the end, don't they? Whoo<u>pee</u> and t<u>ree</u>. Can anyone think of another rhyme?" The answer came quickly from Jon, who laughed as he said, "Miss Pratt is a cat." Peter added quickly, "The cat caught a rat."

Nonsense, which may be doggerel rhyme, is fun. Regardless of the age level, if the setting is one of easy acceptance on the part of the teacher, if the environment is a fairly free one, and if spontaneity is encouraged, the door is open for nonsense rhyming. Nonsense rhymes are not to be equated with poetry, but their role is an important one. When the possibilities of nonsense have been explored, and rhymes combining nonsense with meaning have been created, many children move rather easily into the rhythm of free-flowing verse writing. For some, nonsense is important; for others, less so. But all children should have the experience.[3]

Doggerel Rhyme and Nonsense

The third grader who does not want to be a "sissy," but who is at the developmental stage where incongruities are uproariously funny, may respond to "Biffington Bopp"[4] with:

> *Herman's a burnin'*
> *And he needs turnin'*

---

[3]See Pratt, "Whoopee, I'm a Tree."
[4]Clark Emery, "Biffington Bopp" in Jerome Wyckoff (ed.), *The Golden Grab Bag* (New York: Simon and Schuster, 1951), p. 12.

He has responded to the nonsense rhyme with one of his own.

The less inhibited children answer more freely to nonsense sylla-bles which tend to convey sense impressions. For instance, the teacher said, in a singsong voice,

> *Itsky, bitsky boo*
> *Itsky, mitsky moo*

and Joan answered,

> *Itsky, fitsky foo.*

Almost immediately, Joe said, more slowly, "I'm here, too." Joe was responding with some semblance of meaning, while Joan was caught up in nonsense syllabification and had entered easily into the rhyme-making pattern. Children often begin and the teacher picks it up.

Elsie walked about the first grade room muttering, "Teek, teek, keek, keek" in rhythm. She said the first two quickly, paused, and added the second two. The teacher, who was standing near, said,

> *Teek, teek*
> *Keek, keek.*

She replied in the same rhythm. Elsie smiled and repeated the sylla-bles more audibly. Two other children, painting at an easel nearby, joined. The teacher took rhythm sticks and beat the time. Within five minutes, Elsie, who had also taken rhythm sticks, the two other children, who were beating the rhythm with paint brushes at the easel, and three of Elsie's close friends, who had also picked up rhythm sticks, were all tapping the rhythm and chanting the sylla-bles. This continued for about five minutes, until Jimmy suddenly said in the same rhythm,

> *Beat, beat,*
> *Feet, feet.*

The little group began to repeat this, until Bob suddenly laughed and said, from the book table where he was watching,

> *Beat, beat,*
> *Feet, feet,*
> *Just go to your seat.*

Everyone laughed, and the incident ended.

Nonsense rhyming, developed spontaneously, provides an excellent initiation to more serious verse writing which may follow. The sounds should be rhythmic and initiated with syllables so simple in pattern that rhyming is spontaneous to many children, as in the illustration above. Clapping as the syllables are said often helps the more reticent child. Inasmuch as this stage is a nonsense stage, the child for whom English is a second language can participate without self-consciousness.

As an intermediary stage, between nonsense syllables and verse, nonsense rhymes with some semblance of meaning bring responses more quickly from other children. Joe's answer is a case in point. The more serious child frequently responds as Joe did, with some meaning. Gradually, other children do, too.

> *Skipetty, skipetty hop*
> *Skipetty, skipetty hop*
> *Flipetty, slipetty flop*
> *Flipetty, flipetty flop*

is likely to call forth "shop," "pop," "mop," or "stop" as endings for the next rhyme, such as "Off and away to the shop." First, second, and third graders, especially, thoroughly enjoy this. In the first grade, the emphasis should be on hearing the sounds and rhymes because reading may be too hard for some to fully participate. After listening carefully, children are quick to respond. Some rhyme more easily than others. Incidentally, those who never rhyme should not be urged. When and if ready, they will join.

Fourth, fifth, and sixth graders can read and hear distinctions more easily. If the first four lines are on the chalkboard, the teacher can write down final lines as fast as they are suggested. In the case of children who read and write easily—by fifth or sixth grade, if not before—several sets of nonsense lines may be distributed on mimeographed sheets. Space should be left after each so that students may add their own lines. After a few minutes, the teacher can call for volunteers to read theirs aloud. A number should be read, thus encouraging the reticent and moving all the students into the rhythm of what is going on. Those with the most rhythmic syllables or words are easily discernible. Some contributions can be improved on the spot. Usually the other children are quite spontaneous in their help. Occasionally a group begins to chant an especially rhythmic verse. If this does not come spontaneously, the teacher can suggest, "Let's say Colleen's with her."

> *Timpy, timpy too,*
> *Whimpy, whimpy whoo,*
> *Mimpy, mumpy moo*
> *Cows do it, too.*

Another suggestion leads to simple choral speaking, "Let's all say the first three lines and let Colleen say the fourth." This, of course, can be continued with small groups saying the first, second, and third lines while Colleen says the fourth. Usually other solo speakers produce additional individual fourth lines.

A relaxed atmosphere and a spontaneous, cheerful teacher are conducive to nonsense and doggerel rhyme writing. The fun in the situation is contagious! The level of humor is important. Situations in which the usual in daily activity is upset and in which the daily expectations of people about other people and things are not as usual are hilarious to six, seven, and eight year olds. Verses like the following begin to appear after plenty of syllable rhymes:

> *Neigh, neigh, neigh,*
> *Neigh, neigh, hooray,*
> *Neigh, neigh, today*
> *The horse will play.*
>
> *Round, round, round,*
> *Round, round, round,*
> *Went the bus wheels.*
> *Round, round, round,*
> *Mr. Jones sat on his heels.*
> *Round, round, round*
> *I know how he feels.*
> *Round, round, round,*
> *Went the bus wheels.*

A six year old will laugh at a person who slides and sits down suddenly from his usual upright position.

> *Mr. Smith went down the street,*
> *He slid off his feet,*
> *Gee whiz, said he,*
> *I'm sitting under a tree.*

The young child's concern for a possible broken bone is missing unless the possibility is indicated. By third and fourth grade transposed objects related to people are much appreciated. *The Five*

Hundred Hats of Bartholomew Cubbins,[5] for instance, is not usually fully appreciated at age six, but it is at eight. Or, to refer again to "Biffington Bopp," the refrain is usually very funny to an eight year old, but silly to an eleven year old. A six year old frequently accepts it passively.

Edward Lear's *A Nonsense Alphabet* has a place, expecially from third grade up.

> A was an ape,
> Who stole some white tape,
> And tied up his toes
> In four beautiful bows.
> A funny old ape.[6]

Although the alphabet may appeal to younger ones, children of about eight and older tend to replicate the nonsense.

> *P was for Peter*
> *Who sat on a heater,*
> *And burned his seater,*
> *Poor burnt Peter.*

This is not likely to come from a child younger than eight or nine.

Lear's limericks,[7] too, frequently cause a spontaneous series of nonsense, such as:

> *There was a young boy with some hair,*
> *Whose friends thought he was a bear,*
> *He scratched on a log for some ants,*
> *But, they came and ran up his pants,*
> *And he got big splinters for fair.*

Listening and hearing correctly is important at all ages. Though rhyme comes more easily to some children than to others, when he hears it, and is encouraged to say what is written or said, the child is often caught up in the pattern of it. When the rhyme is repeated

---

[5]Dr. Seuss, *The Five Hundred Hats of Bartholomew Cubbins* (New York: The Vanguard Press, Inc., 1939).

[6]Lear, *Nonsense Books,* p. 219. By permission of the administrators of Constance S. Ester Rosa Cipelletti Lady Strachey deceased.

[7]See also Leland B. Jacobs (ed.), *Funny Folks in Limerick Land* (Champaign, Ill.: Garrard Publishing Co., 1971); and Leland B. Jacobs (ed.), *Animal Antics in Limerick Land* (Champaign, Ill.: Garrard Publishing Co., 1971).

clearly and distinctly several times, the more reticent child often finds participation easier and then will state a rhyme of his own.

Evaluation should be spontaneous judgment primarily as to what rhymes well, what has a rhythm most close to the line with which it is to rhyme, and what almost seems to say itself. Older children, from ages ten to twelve, are sometimes too critical. At this age, too, they sometimes tend toward the rhyme or verse that is too pat and mechanical.

Sensory Appeal

Sensory appeals can be utilized. For example a first grade teacher said, "Listen to the second graders practicing their dance upstairs. What sounds do we hear?" (The first grade had witnessed the practice on the preceding day.) The children's responses included:

> *Rattlety, rattlety, rat,*
> *Rattlety, rattlety, rat,*
> *Clattetty, clattetty, clat.*
>
> *Rattlety, rattlety, rat,*
> *Rattlety, rattlety, rat,*
> *Their feet go tat, tat.*
>
> *Slide, slide, bump, bump,*
> *Slide, slide, thump, thump.*

On the following day, the third example was written on the chalkboard, and read by the teacher and the child who had contributed it originally. Then the teacher asked the child, "Mary, can you do it while you say it?" Mary went slide, slide sideways, and then hopped up and down, as she said, "bump, bump" and "thump, thump." Then the teacher said, "Let's all clap as Mary sings and moves." After this, the children made other suggestions which were followed. A tom tom could have been used as accompaniment. Such activities combine rhythm and rhyme as a more complete bodily activity than merely speaking.

Thus the procedure discussed in chapter 2 was reversed. The bodily movement was second to the rhyming. Actually, with preschool children especially, the bodily movement is more likely to precede verbalization. In the case of first grader Mary, however, verbal communication was well established. Combining rhythm and rhyme freed the rhyme and made it more spontaneous. Even more important, it involved the participation of her classmates. One has only to watch striking pickets, rock festivals, or even sing-alongs to note how easily rhythm and rhyme complement and sustain each other.

A second grade teacher asked, "If we listen, what can we hear?" "Jimmy chewing pellets," came the answer. Everyone listened to the guinea pig, as he crunched the hard pellets.

> *Tht, tht, tht,*
> *Tht, tht, tht,*
> *Crunch, crunch, crunch,*
> *Tht, tht, tht,*
> *Munch, munch, munch*

came from that. The next day, Carolyn looked at Jimmy and said,

> *Crunch, crunch, crunch,*
> *Go Jimmy's teeth,*
> *Munch, munch, munch,*
> *As he wiggles his shiny head,*
> *Shiny, shiny, like a light.*

Rhythm and nonsense had led Carolyn to the beginnings of imaginative verse. The spontaneity of the situation was conducive to Carolyn's own creative expression.

A large, humorous illustration or an enlarged cartoon can be described in nonsense syllables, and sometimes in words. A large picture of Snoopy on his back on his dog house led to:

> *Snoopy, Snoopy,*
> *Poopy, poopy,*
> *Snoopy, Snoopy,*
> *Poop, poop.*

and

> *Szz, szz,*
> *Snore, snore,*
> *Szz, szz,*
> *Pheeewww.*
> *Snoopy, Snoopy,*
> *Sleepy, sleepy dog.*
> *Snoopy, Snoopy,*
> *Snorey dog.*

This kind of nonsense rhyming and play with words and syllables led to more meaningful rhymes and statements, later. Examples are:

> *S stands for Snoopy*
> *Snoopy is goopy.*
> *Slept all the time*
> *Szz, szz, szz.*

and

> *Snoopy sleeps so quiet,*
> *Like a snowy day,*
> *When you can't hear anything*
> *On the street.*

Imagery was used by this child. Later, the same child said,

> *Snow, on a snowy day,*
> *Falls as quiet*
> *As my kitten breathing.*

Sensory musical experiences are discussed in another chapter. In terms of nonsense, however, it may be said that listening to the musical rhythms of sharp, staccato, or of uneven nature may result in nonsense. The third grade listened to *The Parade of the Wooden Soldiers.*[8]

"Can you make sounds to go with it?" asked the teacher.

> *Ta, ta, bump, bump, bump,*
> *Ta, ta, bump, bump, bump,*
> *Ta, ta, bump, bump, bump, bump, bump-a-bump*

said Bill. Then he repeated it, and as the last line said,

> *Ta ta, bump, bump, bump, I go jump, jump.*
> *With a mump, mump, mump,*

added Peter. Carey quickly said,

> *A man with a mump, mump, mump,*
> *Had feet that went jump, jump, jump,*
> *Oh, my, he was a gump, gump.*

Everyone laughed and numerous rhymes were made with "gump." In fact, this led to:

---

[8]Victor Herbert, *The Parade of the Wooden Soldiers,* Victor Record V 25B.

> *Big Gump, who went stump, stump, stump,*

and

> *Little Gump, who went jump, jump, jump.*

The free spirit of rhyming began to add rhythm to much that was said. There is a retention of flowing expression in many cases. After several weeks of such rhyming, one sixth grader wrote,

> *Flowing, flowing, flowing down the hill,*
> *Water, water never still.*
> *Swirling, twirling in the sun,*
> *Brooks are happy in their fun.*

While this is not great poetry, the development and transition from nonsense to what is more serious has retained rhythm and some fluidity of expression. Such creativity, too, tends to move to the realm of more personal experience. Thus it can open the way for more deeply individual expression which may have been blocked and/or self-consciously protected. The free making of nonsense rhymes, even in the form of doggerel, is one of the ways to develop creative poetic expression.

Individual Experience and Inner Feelings

Experiences and encouragement in stating or in otherwise expressing the feelings accompanying them invite the child to sum up his activities verbally. The teacher uses these as a bank from which to draw out the creative expression of each child. As has been indicated above, nonsense rhyming and doggerel verse can develop into poetic verse. The cheerful atmosphere and fun of nonsense encourages children. Many children seize upon the fun of nonsense and move from there on to more imaginative or serious verse writing. When they do, they tend to carry the rhythm of free-flowing expression into the more serious verse forms.

Bodily rhythm can be stirred to expression through other art forms, as was described before, and can be utilized as a precursor to nonsense writing, providing the other art forms are in the same vein. Debussy's *L'Aprés Midi d'un Faun,*[9] for instance, could not be expected to lead to nonsense or fun, whereas Grieg's *In the Hall of the*

---

[9]Claude Debussy, *L'Aprés Midi d'un Faun,* Columbia record 6754.

Mountain King[10] might. The young child tends to make whole body responses, which may be rhythmic expression which can be stated creatively in words. When nonsense is in the atmosphere and the environment, the creative writing generated can be clearly expressive. The child's humor and spontaneity are happy feelings which are expressed in the shared fun.

THE TEACHER'S ROLE

Encouragement and an atmosphere that is free enough to lead to spontaneous creativity are two major factors in any creative writing situation. Add a few ingredients which lend themselves to nonsense, and the environment is set. The children bring their experience, their feelings, and their natural love of nonsense into such a class situation. With an appreciative teacher the stage is set.

Children appreciate different types of fun, humor, and nonsense at different levels, and the teacher must be aware of this. A group of four year olds listen very solemnly to *Susie Mariar*[11] and are unmoved and almost expressionless, while five year olds may comment about her trials and tribulations. Some six year olds, though, are likely to think this rhyme tale somewhat funny. By third grade, Susie's adventures are appreciated; and by fifth and sixth grade, she is called silly and stupid. These derogatory comments usually lead to no positive follow-through.

Thus it is evident that the teacher's judgment helps to determine what materials can be utilized to encourage rhythm and rhyme. She must be aware, too, of what literary materials to introduce or to have available in the class library. With this, she should know what type of nonsense syllables, words, and phrases will be likely to hold the most appeal. A knowledge of children's literature and of child development is indispensable. The same things simply are not funny to children of all ages. The appeal to fun and the feelings so generated are indispensable for a rhyming experience.

The teacher with courage to try some of the preceding suggestions, with perception enough to analyze whether she is succeeding, and with genuine enough interest to understand and to evaluate the process itself and the children's responses may develop genuine creativity through these means. She will enjoy the pleasure of greater creativity in teaching, too, as a result.

---

[10]Edvard Grieg, *In the Hall of the Mountain King,* RCA Victor record 147.
[11]For one version, see Lois Lenski, *Susie Mariar* (New York: Henry Z. Walck Publishers, 1967).

Growing awareness in noting possible relevant materials will add zest to what is done. The teacher will notice, too, that all sorts of things hitherto passed over can be generating factors for fun and creativity.

Loosening the "tight child" requires patient and often quiet, unobtrusive encouragement. To know which device to use and when to share the first hesitantly made contributions requires skill. As a general rule of thumb, it is usually wise to ask the quiet child's permission to share what he has produced. The outgoing, more lively and active child's contribution can usually be shared immediately. Group choral reading of much that is done is frequently a useful equalizer. The hesitant child usually finds himself participating, almost without being aware of it. At the same time, the child whose nonsense has led almost immediately to personal poetic form should have his need for privacy respected. Contributions should be made and accepted from all, eventually. Needless to say, pressure is of no help at all and there should be none of it.

The foreign-speaking child may be able to express nonsense but in another language. If someone present can understand it, it is wise to take it down in the original first. A translation may then be made. Nonsense syllabification often enables the non-English-speaking child to participate. In such instances, there is no language problem.

The nonsense syllables and rhymes given in the illustrations in this chapter were initiated by both teacher and children. These are not usually the kind of nonsense rhymes circulated by children among themselves. In their study, the Opies hold that variations of phraseology apparently occur more by accident than by design, and seem to come about by mishearing and misunderstanding. However, they are adapted in terms of local conditions.[12] These researchers divide oral rhymes into two classes: those essential to the regulation of games and relationships and those which are expressions of exuberance.[13]

It seems wisest for the teacher to steer away from attempts to reform traditional rhymes; she should work with spontaneous original syllable combinations and rhymes. Most of the nonsense with which the teacher works would tend to be in the Opies' second classification. Exuberant expressions, accompanying chants, and on-the-spot jingles and rhymes provide plenty of material. It is *original* expression that can lead to creative poem making. When individual chil-

---

[12]Iona Opie and Peter Opie, *The Lore and Language of Schoolchildren* (London: Oxford University Press, 1961), p. 8.

[13]*Ibid.*, p. 17.

dren do recite traditional rhymes in traditional or adapted forms, they may be accepted for what they are (unless, of course, of the derogatory variety). Occasionally, something like "Mary, Mary/ Quite contrary " may be recited with an ending invented on the spot. This could lead into further invention. However, since the first two lines set the pattern of the rhythm and rhyme, they are not original and tend to govern what follows. Also, the ending may be quite negative. On the other hand,

> *Whoopee,*
> *I'm a tree*

is original. It is exuberant expression and can lead to further creativity without any restriction but what it is in itself—a child's expression made up on the spot!

VERSE AND POETRY

In the first section of this chapter, we have considered the role of nonsense and how a transition from such nonsense to verse writing can be developed. This does not imply that every child necessarily develops into a creator of verse and poetry through this medium. What it does mean is that enough children can profit from this technique to make it genuinely worthwhile. One caution should be noted: for the child for whom nonsense has no appeal, this approach should not be urged. However, it is quite possible that such a child may need help in finding out what fun can be had from such activities!

A number of children, regardless of whether or not nonsense is important to them, put their feelings into words more or less poetic in form because they express a mood or describe some object or event with depth of feeling and in words which flow in rhythm. I agree with Huck and Kuhn that if poetry "demands total response from the individual—his intellect, senses, emotion, and imagination," it invites its hearers to participate in the experience rather than to tell about it.[14] Some children frequently seem to speak in poetry instead of prose.

> *The leaf came down*
> *Soft as the footsteps*

---

[14]Charlotte Huck and Doris Kuhn, *Children's Literature in the Elementary School* (New York: Holt, Rinehart and Winston, Inc., 1968), p. 386.

Of a kitten stepping
On the grass

said Lisa, as she turned from watching the leaf fall. Later, when Mrs. Jones read this to the third graders, Lisa smiled and said, "A kitten steps so softly on the grass that she's never told to stay off."

Mrs. Jones asked, "How many of you noticed the leaves blowing down?" Several of the children had.

Ursula said, "Maybe Lisa thought it was like her cat, but the leaves from that big tree [a cottonwood] sail down more like pieces of cloth. I suppose they really blow, but they look to me as through they were sailing."

"I saw some start down and go back up a ways," said Ben.

"Yeah, air currents do it," Bob said sagely.

"Maybe those from that elm tree," commented Don, "were what Lisa saw. They do come more quietly. I think that they are like fish swimming through the air!"

"Brown fish," added Sue. "Brown rustly fish swimming to the ground after they look around."

"Ground-round! Ha," laughed Pete, "Sue, you made a rhyme— ground and round!"

The discussion may seem to have gotten nowhere! Mrs. Jones had let it wander, noting which children participated, and what was said. She looked up. "Well," she smiled, "you seem to be reminded of many things by leaves as they fall. You have mentioned a kitten, pieces of cloth, and fish."

"And," said Pete, "boats—canoes are more like it—from the elm."

"All right, Pete," said Mrs. Jones, "we can certainly add boats. Now," she added, "you have said that they *came* down, that they *sail* down, that they *start* down and *go* back, that they *swim,* and we did mention *blow.* We'll look again, tomorrow." Mrs. Jones said no more. During the next morning's playground period, however, she noted that several children were watching the leaves fall.

During the days that followed, she received five verses about leaves. Typical of these:

Sailing down, sailing down,
The elm leaf like a canoe
Fell on the ground
Near me and you.

It should be recognized that, although Mrs. Jones led the first discussion, she did not dominate it. Neither did she applaud the efforts of some children. She merely led the children to add to what she had presented from one of them. Then she summarized what the children had said. This was what the leaves were like and what their movement had reminded the children of. Mrs. Jones chose the subject and the motion-function aspect of what was seen and stated.

Nouns and verbs are the two foci of young children. They look at the subject and what it does. As most people realize, activity, function, and motion, in general, appeal to the youngest. Long descriptive phrases, alliteration, and much imagery are not usually used by children under eight years of age. Following Lisa's reference to the kitten, Mrs. Jones sought to see just what the leaf reminded the children of. Then she summarized the verbs used to tell how the leaves had come down. Simple—yet it was enough to encourage the eight year olds to add new possibilities to their creative expressions. For the children who really "saw" the leaf swim like a fish, this experience was added to their growing fund of experiences of leaves in autumn. This fund might be drawn upon later when, in a burst of feeling in response to some autumn scene, the child created a new verse.

Despite the special interest in the subject and what it does, imagery does develop. Some children use it more frequently than others. Imagery in poetry is grasped in concept by around age ten, according to Flora Arnstein.[15] However, I have found that some very young children do use it. For instance, the four year old trying to describe the state of his fingers said, "They're sticky-sticky like a jelly apple." However, it is best not to center on imagery until second or third grade, because its use is too likely to be forced and unnatural before that time. This does not mean you should neglect evidence of the use of imagery. Rather, uses of it should be carefully recorded, remembered, accepted.

All adults have heard the rhymed endings forced by some children. As Arnstein states, "When children employ rhyme, they are driven into the most absurd ineptitudes." She adds that "the poems in which rhymes occur are invariably trivial."[16] While young children's rhymes are often absurd, I do not agree that the poems are necessarily trivial. Rejection of the rhyme need not be as complete as Arnstein seems to feel, though rhymes do need to be watched and other forms encouraged. The deadly rhythm and unnatural superficial endings may come anyway. However, they are less likely to

---

[15]Flora Arnstein, *Poetry in the Elementary Classroom* (New York: Appleton-Century-Crofts, 1962), pp. 94-95.

[16]*Ibid.*

appear if the experiences are shared, if the teacher is receptive to the poetic whenever it appears, and if she requires no rigid assignments for written verse (which sometimes force children who then force rhyme endings). Also, not stressing the importance of rhyme helps when children seem especially prone to force endings.

In one case the kindergarten teacher in a housing project carried through an experience similar to that of Mrs. Jones. Her five year olds were watching the traffic on a raised highway which ran near their playyard.

"Zippetty, look at that big truck," exclaimed Tyrone. "Man, that's like a plane, it goes so fast."

"Huh," said Raymond, "that ain't no plane. Man, that's a *truck*. Ax me."

"Yeah," said Tyrone.

Miss Burgess, who was listening said, "But, Raymond, it is going awfully fast!"

"Yeah," said Raymond.

"Man, you ain't never seen such a fast one," said Tyrone emphatically.

"What else goes fast?" asked Miss Burgess. By this time, several other children had gathered near her. The responses to her question included a subway, a horse, an army plane, a rocket ship. The children continued to watch the traffic on the highway.

Two days later, Tyrone said, when the group was in the room, sitting down for the mid-morning snack, "I seen my big truck again. Man, oh man, it zipped down like a silver space ship. Awful fast, and fast, and fast. A big silver space ship."

Miss Burgess wrote this down and read it to the group again later. After that, Raymond said,

> *A silver space ship*
> *Silver space ship*
> *It sailed along to the Bronx.*

Elinor said softly, and somewhat hesitantly,

> *Sailing, sailing,*
> *A silver space ship*
> *Was a truck*
> *Faster and faster*
> *Sailing down the highway.*

Miss Burgess' class was beginning to "speak" poetry, if we grant the children a real experience, intensity of feeling, some thought about what was stated, and the use of rhythmic expression.

While there are numerous approaches to encourage children (not only to be creative and to express their feelings), some seem to be more productive of beginning verse than others. From about age seven to age nine or ten, the following device may bring forth a jingle or a verse. The teacher, well aware of the children's fondness for nonsense, of their need for ego strength and identity, and of their quickness in reciting short rhymes and jingles may give them, "There was a . . ."

> *There was a small boy named Jack*
> *Who carried a great big pack*
> *Now do you suppose*
> *It was full of clothes*
> *That pack of the boy named Jack?*

Certain children usually seize upon this approach immediately. Names, other children, pets, objects, and almost anything else can be open to their rhymed verse. Frequently these poems are two or three lines in length, but they may go on for ten or twelve lines. Usually begun by one child, a verse may be finished by the same child or one or more of his classmates. The wise teacher knows that this kind of verse requires a kind of quick perception—quite different from that exhibited when the children watched the falling leaves.

> *There was a boy named Moe*
> *Who stubbed his great big toe,*
> *"Ouch," cried the boy named Moe.*

Two books with selections chosen by Leland Jacobs add greatly to this type of approach.

Stop!

A careless young driver, McKissen
Just never would stop, look, and listen
A train at great speed
He gave not one heed
Now lissen! McKissen is missin.[17]

---

[17]Lee Blair, "Stop!" in Jacobs (ed.), *Funny Folks in Limerick Land.* Reprinted with permission. See also Jacobs (ed.), *Animal Antics in Limerick Land.*

This is not formal poetry, but such verse does have a place in creative writing. I tend to agree with the distinction made by Huck and Kuhn that imagination and depth of emotion are both qualities that distinguish poetry from verse.[18] Elizabeth Coatsworth's distinction, which they quote, is relevant. She refers to rhyme as "poetry in petticoats."[19] Each of these has a place in the classroom and the teacher should receive each as it is given.

Another and probably more common approach is for the teacher to choose some section from a child's written or oral composition. She writes it on the chalkboard, stating that it sounds like poetry, which in itself may be enough to encourage various additions.

"The ball rolled, like a red flash, to the gutter. Then it bounced up and down in the murky, muddy water." This is not genuine poetry, but Miss White told her fifth grade that it might be rewritten like this:

> *The ball rolled like*
> *A red flash to the gutter*
> *Then, it bobbed up and down*
> *In the murky, muddy water.*

She immediately received a number of suggestions. Eventually her class members produced:

> *The ball slid like*
> *A streak all red*
> *To the gutter, and straight ahead*
> *Where it bobbed down and up*
> *Like it was in a cup,*
> *While the muddy water went ahead.*

Not poetry, but verse. This fifth grade was on the way to verse writing.

Collaboration by members of the class on one poem has been mentioned throughout this book. Koch makes several workable suggestions which might be mentioned here. He suggests the "I Wish ..." poem which is initiated by having each child write one line beginning with "I wish" and including certain other items such as a color, a comic strip character, and a city or country. After the chil-

---

[18]Huck and Kuhn, *Children's Literature,* pp. 386-87.
[19]Elizabeth Coatsworth, *The Sparrow Bush* (New York: W. W. Norton & Company, Inc., 1966), p. 8.

dren pass these in, Koch reads them in turn as one poem.[20] However, it seems that it would have been just as feasible to have had each child continue individually to elaborate on what he wishes.

Arnstein speaks of enumeration, and "I like ..." She holds that children do enumerate and mentions this technique in relation to seven and eight year olds.[21] It does appear at different times in the expression of young children. In creative writing, when the teacher gives attention to enumeration, it can broaden creative possibilities. It also tends to focus attention on one item. If all the animals in the zoo are enumerated, the list serves as a summary and keeps attention on the zoo. In a more specialized way, all kinds of cats, for instance, may be mentioned.

Haiku

In recent years, Haiku writing has intrigued some adults and fascinated children in the middle and upper grades. If children are unacquainted with this form, the teacher can introduce it. For instance, she might bring in a large snail and read:

> A red morning sky
> For you, snail;
> Are you glad about it?[22]

Or, holding some flowers, so that the children can see the petals,

> Stillness:
> The sound of the petals
> Sifting down together.[23]

An excellent way to begin, if possible, is to wait for some natural event such as a sudden shower or the first snow. Have the children watch it. Then, get several to describe it briefly:

> *The snow, so white*
> *Falls shortly to the dark earth.*

---

[20]Kenneth Koch, *Wishes, Lies, and Dreams* (New York: Vintage Books/Chelsea House Publishers, 1970), p. 64. See also pp. 5, 86.

[21]Arnstein, *Poetry in the Elementary Classroom*, pp. 46-47.

[22]Issa, in R. H. Blyth (ed.), *Haiku*, Vol. 3, p. 245. © Hallmark Cards, Inc. Reprinted by permission of Hokuseido Press, Tokyo, and Hallmark Cards, Inc.

[23]Chora, in R. H. Blyth (ed.), *Haiku*, Vol. 2, p. 361. © Hallmark Cards, Inc. Reprinted by permission of Hokuseido Press, Tokyo, and Hallmark Cards, Inc.

> *Snowflakes stars in white*
> *Dropping to sleep on the ground.*

The second has the correct number of syllables, while one needs to be added to the first line of the first. When asked, the children may want to say it differently, "The snow soft and white." How do you feel about it? Sixth graders might be asked, "Do you feel any particular way? Might the earth? Has a mood been created by the first two lines?" When asked to describe the feeling or mood briefly, the following were stated:

> *Sleeping and covered*

and

> *White world so silent.*

When the teacher asked whether the first might be made even shorter, the "so" was removed. Then she added one of these lines, letting the children decide which was to be added to which pair of first lines. Thus, the results were:

> *The snow soft and white*
> *Falls softly to the dark earth*
> *Sleeping and covered.*

and

> *Snowflakes, stars in white*
> *Dropping to sleep on the ground*
> *White world so silent.*

Remember, these two were developed from a chalkboard full of the children's suggestions! The teacher then told the class that they had created two Haiku. He explained what Haiku were and that, in the original Japanese, each verse is seventeen syllables and written in three lines. The fact that the pattern is five syllables in the first and third lines and seven in the second intrigued some and seemed restrictive to other children. However, a number of children began to write their own Haiku. Thus another form of creative writing was added.

The Friday Box

Many of the same ways suggested to develop creative writing, in general, may be used for creative poetry writing. Jingles, limericks, free verse, rhymes and rhymed verse, ballads, and Haiku are varied enough in form to provide some outlet for almost any child. Inasmuch as the feelings expressed in poems are likely to be heightened and may be considerably more personal, the wise teacher suggests ways of submission which are acceptable to the shyest child.

Some of the ways to insure the child of privacy are:

1. A large covered box, with a slit in the cover, is kept in a place which assures some privacy, such as on a corner table or on the teacher's desk. It may be labeled and decorated by the children.

2. A large envelope is given to each child and he places it on the teacher's desk when he wishes to submit a poem in it. It is placed in another location when the teacher is ready to return it.

3. A small notebook, especially labeled, is kept by each child and submitted when he has an addition. This is then returned.

4. A box, or other receptacle, is called the Friday Box (or Monday, etc.) and brought out on the designated day. The poems are then put into it by those who wish to do so.

At first, it is best to suggest that work may be submitted anonymously, if the child wishes. This will encourage the most reticent. Within a short time, the majority will sign their poems, and usually want to share them with their classmates. They should not be read aloud unless permission is granted by the child. The teacher's comments should be brief and encouraging, especially at first.

4

From Six to Eight, What Do We Appreciate?

How to develop creative verbal expression with children from six through eight years of age.

From six to eight, many things are appreciated! Briefly and generally speaking, the six year old tends to rebel against controls—much as he did at four—in order to test his growing powers as well as those of adult and school authority. The child often has grandiose schemes which struggle for formulation and recognition. Reformulation, with adult guidance, aids the children in achieving satisfaction. For instance, some first graders who wanted to construct a two-story house with chimney in the classroom were satisfied when the teacher helped them to find out that a one-story house complete with chimney could be built. Similarly, once a child can write, he may plot long tales which he is unable to complete due to lack of the perfected physical skill and lack of an attention span long enough for him to follow through to a conclusion. The wise teacher estimates the attention span and the child's ability, physically, to write. Then he helps him achieve satisfaction either through a tape recorder or a shorter written story.

At age six, the emotional hurts that frequently cause more tears than physical bumps can be channeled into positive achievements based on developing feelings. "I cried, Marilyn didn't let me see her ring. I like Marilyn. Tuesday I will see her ring."

Appreciation by the teacher and by his peers is important to a six year old. Six year olds can work and play well in small groups of their own choosing. Whole class activities receive earnest concentration and participation for periods of growing length. From fifteen or twenty minutes in September to over an hour by June are not uncommon lengths of time for social interchange and cooperative activities participated in by the whole class. The free choice of companions begins to be same-sex oriented by age six and a half. "The boys played ball in the park. The girls did not play ball. I threw a curve."

The new role of being part of a whole school and feelings of superiority over the preschoolers, now left behind, bring new self-assertiveness. Some of these feelings can be found in the creative activities of first graders.

Seven, again speaking generally, tends to be a calmer age. Some of the learnings of the preceding year need to be consolidated. The child enjoys his friends, his activities, and his new-found powers. Recognizing this, the teacher needs to be aware of the tendency some seven year olds have to be complacent and to "float along" on the acceptance their peers show of them and which they, in turn, make. Social adjustment is easier now and most children have one or more close friends. Give-and-take experiences should be expanding seven year olds' horizons, although the teacher needs to watch that early cliques are not restrictive to interests and activities. While much learning is a continuation of that of the preceding years, the wise teacher plans new and different group experiences to keep her children aware of the ever-widening activities of which they are capable. Imagination does occasionally need stirring by the new and dynamic, so that the old retains its place, but so that the new and developing aspects of creativity are assured. A longer span of interest enables the seven year old to carry out creative work of greater scope than he was capable of at age six.

The more fully developed coordination of their small muscles enables seven year olds to perform physical activities requiring finer controls. Inasmuch as they have been in school for several years in some cases, their attendance may be much better due to having had many childhood diseases and to having gained greater immunity against colds. Thus the possibilities for sustained activities are again greater.

By age eight, friendships are of greater durability, plans can be carried out more easily, and cooperative enterprises can be considerably more complicated. It seems at times as though all the third grade teacher has to do is to supply materials. Actually, of course, she needs to aid in the development of new interests as indicated, to judge which seem possible and valuable enough to encourage over long-term periods, and to be supportive of new manifestations of individual prowess. The growing interest in folk and fairy tales, for instance, and in individual figures who perform lends depth and breadth to creative writing about golden-haired princesses and swashbuckling heroes. Statements of identification with beauty, with strength, and with winning should be written down. The clear-cut all good or all bad nature of such characters can serve the child as suggestions for his own "most good" and "most evil." The "ought" for behavior becomes clearer. The child's plans may begin to indicate individual sacrifice and daring, which, though not carried through too often, do reflect development of additional feelings and interests. These interests and feelings begin to form the bases for much creative writing.

Some children can plan and carry through individual projects of their own devising. For instance, Danny planned, printed in manuscript, and displayed his own newspaper daily for several weeks until his teacher induced him to incorporate other third graders in his project.

FREEDOM AND MECHANICS

The emphasis in creative writing for these children, as for others, is on the expression of the child's personal feeling, on freedom from stereotypic phrases, and upon developing verbal expression in writing which is distinctly the individual's own. Critical thinking on the child's part should not be encouraged until the initial expression of feeling is recorded, if truly creative writing is to result.

As at any age, freedom is necessary for creativity. Yet the mechanics of form must eventually become the child's own skills. While both freedom and grammatical skills need to be developed, the latter must neither dominate nor restrict the former. While freedom receives priority in creative writing, structure is not be to ignored. Writing which is completely free of structure does not communicate. Judge *after* the words are written. The student's final formulation should combine both free expression of feeling and the critical thoughts and ideas of the writer. All too often, cultural, communal, or familial "oughts" interfere, letting stereotypic, conventional forms result. *Creative writing* means what it says. I, as an individual, originate written work which is the image of what I *feel*.

Unfortunately, in creative writing, the raw material, namely that which is felt,[1] is too often repressed almost to the point of nonexistence. In such cases, the critical powers have little or no raw materials upon which to work.

A six year old tells gaily what happened: "My dog barked because my aunt brought her cat and then he wanted to play with it and then he went out with my Father and-ah ..." "And" and "and-ah" are the connecting links between what is being stated and new thoughts and feelings, as they appear. Six year olds can, and in some cases do, go on indefinitely!

Freedom to tell? Of course! When the desire is for creativity, writing must be delayed for a time. However, children of age six turning seven, seven, and eight can write down much of what they say. At times, though, the tape recorder or the teacher with the ready pencil are necessary, or much would be lost.

In one classroom, Amelia related a number of things which cer tered mainly about her dog. After five minutes of narration, Mrs. Neir spoke softly, appreciatively, but firmly. "That's an interesting story, Amelia. I think that we had better hear the rest of it tomorrow." Then she added, "Amelia, you've told us many things about what your dog does, but we do not know what he looks like. Can you tell us?"

"He's black and his name is Tiger," said Amelia.

"Fine," said Mrs. Neir, "but I have seen many black dogs. How would any of us know Tiger?"

"He's shiny black, shiny like - like black glass. He's shiny like the black glass table my aunt has," said Amelia.

"Shiny like black glass helps," said Mrs. Neir. "Is there anything else?"

"He's brave, brave like a tiger," said Amelia, "and that is why he is named Tiger."

"Fine," said Mrs. Neir. "Brave is a quality that is fine. Is he brave in any special way?"

"He fights with big dogs when they come into the yard," said Amelia.

Thus Mrs. Neir slowly drew out what Amelia meant, and by means of how and what questions, caused the little girl to clarify what she had said. Many creative writers assume too much of the reader. Amelia's narration was not hurt by the questions because they were completely within the context of what she was telling. Mrs. Neir, by

---

[1] Feeling, in turn, stems from individual interaction in previous experiences.

her questions, drew out Amelia's particular description. Through this process, Amelia's narration meant more to her listeners and was more individual.

The wisdom of strategic questions asked after individual verbal expression is partly responsible for the "show and tell" times which have become an important part of many first graders' daily activities. While this is an excellent way to develop verbal expression, in too many cases it has become so routinized that the initial reason for it tends to be submerged into a habitual mechanism. Many six year olds find it easier to project through the object they are discussing rather than to stand up and just talk extemporaneously. Thus, the "show" part of "show and tell." For example, Luisa rubbed the red beads in her hand gently, as she turned them. "Beads are red. Pretty. Beads from Puerto Rico," she said shyly.

Mrs. Rubero smiled. "Yes, Luisa, *the* beads are red. *They* are pretty. Who gave them to you?"

Luisa smiled, "*The* beads from Tia Ana," she said.

In another instance, Ronald grinned shyly, looked down, and then held up a beaded belt. "My belt is an Indian belt. It tells a story. A boy is hunting. He's after buffalo . . ." As Ronald projected himself into his interest in his belt and identified with the boy, he looked up, spoke clearly, and his shyness disappeared in the confidence he gained from telling his friends about his own object of interest. After Ronald's clear and coherent account, Mr. Rubin snapped off the tape recorder, saying, "Fine, Ronald. We have it all, I think. We'll find out when we listen later."

The next morning everyone had a rexographed copy of Ronald's story. Later that day Ronald wrote, "My Indian belt tells a story. The story is about a boy hunting buffalo. The boy was brave."

Although this brief story, written with help with spelling, was short and matter of fact, it was Ronald's own. Ronald's feeling about the belt and the boy came through clearly. Mr. Rubin had said nothing, beyond, "Ronald, we all enjoyed reading the story taken from the tape recorder. Here is some paper. You try to write the story for your book. I'll put the words that you need on the chalk board."

Two months later, Ronald wrote, "Indian boys are brave. They hunt with just a bow and arrow. Some days they spear silvery fish in a big stream all alone." This, too, was Ronald's own. His interest in Indians had been developing, and he was able to make some generalizations.

During the intervening period, Ronald's initial feeling and his special interest had combined with his thoughts and ideas. His feeling was expressed the first time, after which the recorded and rexographed versions gave him an objectification of it. He could see what his feelings had been. He interacted reflectively with his original feelings; his final writing combined both feeling and his critical thoughts and ideas. In the meantime, after the initial expression had been fully stated, the recording or writing down of it made it an object which could be considered in terms of the skills of effective communication. Let's be more explicit about just one phrase. Before the final version, Ronald had written, "They catch fish ..." This phrase had come forth quite spontaneously. Ronald studied the statement for a few minutes and then said, "No, not catch, but 'spear'." With the object of his feeling expressed and written down before him, he could interact on a thinking basis. His feeling and thought were then combined on this particular point.

On the same day that Ronald had brought his belt, Jayney had brought a Vietnamese doll; Ingrid, a picture of herself on a pony; Moe, a small fire boat; and William, a catcher's mit. The follow-up varied, but it did center on each child's item. While the interests of the other children did not all continue as long as Ronald's, William did write several short items about baseball. Also, weeks later, Jayney wrote, "Girls wear pretty dresses in Vietnam. They are pretty like flowers. We wear bright tops and brown slacks."

By the second and third grades, longer stories are being written. With emphasis on his own expression, on how he feels about things, each author makes his story distinctive. Words are written on the chalkboard as needed. Words of general use are called to the attention of the whole class, and some become group spelling words. A complete thought, feeling, or idea is in sentence form. "And-ah" is discouraged and the period stressed. The question mark becomes important, is discussed, and its use learned as the follow-up to John's "Do you know what is in my house? It's a macaw bird."

It is important to note here that grammar and punctuation, as needed, should grow out of the expressed statement made by one or more children. How is what has been said to be made clearer? For instance, how do we show what a question is?

One day, Tom wrote, "My cat is large. He is very black. He is a boy so he won't have kittens. He is strong and can jump from the bookcase. Maybe he will jump up to a tree top some day." Tina wrote, "My cat is small. She is a kitten. She seems to dance on her tiny pink foot pads. She is like a ballet dancer. She is white and as soft as an Angora mitten." Mr. Stein, Tom and Tina's third grade teacher, thought that a group cat story might be worthwhile. Although he knew that too many group stories might limit individual creativity, he realized that a few can be very helpful to focus thoughts, ideas, and feelings as well as to encourage the shy child. The finished story which his class dictated was as follows:

Cats

Cats are big and little.
Some are long-haired.
Cats may be striped or plain black, gray, or white.
Some cats have spots on them.
Cats can have one, two, or three colors.
Cats climb with their claws.
Cats are related to tigers, leopards, and lions.
Joan has a cat from Burma.
Bill has a cat from Siam.
Sue's cat is called an alley cat.
George's is a Persian cat with long hair and Jean's is a
    short-haired cat from Ohio.

During the two weeks that followed, George and Sue each wrote a longer and rather creative story about their cats. Sue described hers as "slinky and black" with feet that "pack a punch" and "teeth like the sharp bit in my father's brace and bit set." George described his as "long and fluffy like cotton candy or my aunt's powder puff." He said that his cat "purred softly like the organ in the church down the block."

Granting that these are but beginnings, each of these children is stating in his own terms just how he feels about a cat. Cats present a common experiential focus for these children. However, children are different and their feelings vary. Their own stories show this. If they all sound identical, more individual attention is indicated. Each child should be encouraged to state what he himself likes, feels, and thinks. While peer group feeling is strong, individuation need not be lost. Once lost, it is very difficult to recreate.

After Mrs. Ryan's first grade returned from their trip to the Botanical Garden, they made an Experience Chart, drew pictures, discussed ways to plant flowers, and did the usual things a class does after a fruitful trip. However, inasmuch as Mrs. Ryan wanted to encourage creative writing, she used special techniques. Her class had shown little evidence of creativity. The children had for the most part come to her room from a very formal kindergarten or had not been in school at all before entering her class. Several were shy children who were recent arrivals to the city. In two cases, children were living with relatives who had been complete strangers to them until very recently. Mrs. Ryan was aware of the effects that these experiences had had on her children.

After the Experience Chart had been dictated, she asked the class to think of the things that they had seen and to remember what each had liked best. *What We Liked Best at the Botanical Garden* was written on the chalkboard. After a few moments, each child was asked what he liked best and this was recorded.

> *Jim liked the tall rubber plants.*
> *Jane liked the purple African violets by the waterfall.*
> *Custer liked the insect-eating plant.*
> *Eloise liked the smell of the rose garden.*
> *Alan liked the tall cactus from Mexico. . . .*

Later, on the same day, after each child had read his choice (with some help), Mrs. Ryan asked each child to think about the thing that he had chosen and to decide about just why he had chosen what he had. These comments were recorded on a tape recorder so that they could be played back.

For instance, Eloise said, "I liked the smell of the rose garden. It was like living in perfume." Alan said, "I liked the tall cactus from Mexico. It made me think of cowboys."

That afternoon the comments were played back and there was some discussion. The next day each child received a copy of his two statements on a dittoed sheet. Later in the day, the children copied these into their notebooks. If they wanted to do so, they added more. For example, Alan's developed as follows:

> *I liked the tall cactus from Mexico. It made me think of*
> *cowboys. Cowboys ride around cactus when they chase a bad*
> *man. The cactus spines are too sharp to put your hand on. They*
> *stick you.*

As a follow-up to the same kind of trip, Mr. Bogan's second grade dictated a class story and then each wrote, *What I Liked Best at the Botanical Garden.* Examples were:

> *I liked the people who sat behind us when we ate lunch. They*
> *gave us candy. They told us how Indians made canoes from*
> *birch bark. We saw birch trees.*

> *I liked the rubber tree. We saw the sap. It is cooked to make rubber.*
>
> *I liked the big red roses. They made me thrilled. They smelled beautiful. My mother has some rose perfume. I put some on myself. I smell like a rose.*

The second graders' dictated class story of their trip was printed in the school newspaper.

Mr. Barlon's third graders planned their trip carefully. They had formulated some questions for which they wanted to find answers. When they returned, each child wrote about the trip. The only suggestions that Mr. Barlon made were that the children were to ask for the spelling of whatever words they needed; they were to keep margins, to choose one or two things that they liked and to say why they liked them. Tyrone wrote:

> *I saw long vines. Tarzan swings from vines like them. I wanted to try to swing on a vine. I want to be Tarzan.*

Antoine wrote:

> *I liked the stone cactus plants. They played a trick on me. Were they real? Yes, they were real plants.*

The next day, Mr. Barlon divided the class into groups of five or six children each. Each group was to plan a short talk to give to another class. The talk was to give the children in the other class some idea of whether or not they might want to make the same trip. One typical group report was:

> *Why should you go to the Botanical Garden? We'll tell you. It's cool and pretty. You see plants like nowhere else. You will see coffee plants with red berries. Coffee is made from them. You will see the tiniest plants in the world. You should go to the Botanical Gardens.*

In each case, there was some group sharing of the follow-up of the trip. There was ample opportunity for individual expression with some help given rather unobtrusively. Each child was given the chance to choose what he wanted to talk and to write about. He was encouraged to state why. To the adult, the results were not startling. It should be noted that each child accepted his own opportunity and that there were few stereotyped answers. By the time these same children reached the sixth grade, their creative writing, which had resulted from similar treatment during the preceding years, was interesting, individual, imaginative, and in some cases it was surprising in its maturity of insight and depth of expression.

ENCOURAGING IMAGINATION

Some children seem to write creatively without too much effort, while others seem so blocked, unimaginative, or hesitant that it is a real struggle for them to write anything of their own. A number of suggestions have been made to help these children.

Rhythm is one help—chanting and then varying the chant. The first grader who kept mumbling "I'm a Mumbo Jumbo" finally finished with "I'm a Mumbo Jumbo, a Sumbo, Sumbo, Lumbo." At least he was playing with sounds! Some stories do have repetitive rhymes—for example, many folk and fairy tales. The child who hears them makes up his own. These can play an important part in the creative writing of a third grader.

Some eight year olds who had been listening daily to their teacher reading *Charlotte's Web*[2] began to discuss animal friends and pets. The teacher led one discussion which centered mainly around the dogs and cats possessed by the children or their friends. The next morning she brought in a young tame guinea pig, Tinker, and said that he could visit for a few days. Pets, and animals in general, took on added dimension. Tinker's sounds were analyzed as "his way of talking." Several children brought in other pets. Two turtles, a mouse, a snail, and a bowl of guppies were added. Several imaginative stories about these living things were written, ranging from a simple "pourquoi" tale about how the father guppy gained his bright colors to a four line verse about the "slow, but steady snail." The teacher said little. However, she carefully enlarged the experiences of her class, and the results were evident in the creative writing.

This type of addition in order to enlarge experience can and needs to be done in various ways. Class trips, individual reports on special events, the well-chosen story read or told by the teacher, occasional films, and discussions by visitors are all helpful. For example, after Father's Day, the second grade teacher found his children full of "what *I* shall do when I'm grown up!" They wrote, told, and made verses about it. This activity had been touched off by having each father state briefly what he did each day as his kind of work.

---

[2]E. B. White, *Charlotte's Web* (New York: Harper and Brothers, 1952).

When any child can say, "It's mine; I did it; I made my own," he has expressed the satisfaction which should be available to all children. The variations are great and the products many! Each has its place and each child the right to achieve his maximum.

WRITING MY STORY

Many children even in first, second, and third grade do write on their own and are creative. They may have real creative talent. Whether or not they do, plenty of opportunity must be given so that the child can write when he wishes and so that he does not feel put on the spot to produce something whether or not he is able to do so. The teacher can help by being certain that pencils and paper are available, by lending an eye or an ear if and when requested, and by keeping a general hands-off policy until the child requests assistance or an audience. The over-aggressive adult has stemmed the creativity of more than one developing writer! Respect the child as an individual. Jane may want to write as much as Jim wants to play ball. If the child wants to write, let her write! Refrain from anything which makes her self-conscious.

When the child wants to write, he may want help. This need may be apparent before he starts, while in process, or when he has finished. A number of nonverbal experiences have been recommended already. One of these may start him off! Some children need to sit quietly and to be alone. One teacher had an "Alone Corner" where children could work by themselves, or just sit. While it was used most frequently for reading, occasionally it was used for writing. Sometimes the child needs to talk after he has been sitting quietly for a time. If so, let him indicate it. He may need some kind of quiet interval and then a "talking out" time before he starts to write.

During the writing, the most usual request is for help in spelling. Occasionally, other requests are made. After he has finished writing, many a child wants to hand what he has written to his teacher with the request not to read it to the class. The writing and the feeling it expresses seem too personal to be shared at this time. Later, after discussion with the teacher, when what has been written has become objectified more fully, when it has cooled a bit, many young writers are happy to read what they have written aloud or to have the teacher read it for them.

When finished, some boys and girls have requests for some specific kind of help such as, "Well, I got them there, then they had the fire, but I can't get it ended," or, "The dog was winning, but I couldn't have him kill the guy and I didn't know just what to do with him." Talking out such problems frequently helps. At other times, if it is acceptable to the author, reading the selection aloud is of real assistance to get to the problem part and to let class members make suggestions. If the atmosphere is congenial, worthwhile assistance is likely to be forthcoming. Some teachers set aside a special time each week, or more often, for a sharing workshop. While this tends to be of more value to fourth, fifth, and sixth graders, it can be a successful practice to use with mature third graders.

One situation to avoid is reading aloud some piece of writing by a very unpopular child. This can be completely devastating, because the class may use the writing as an object upon which to pour the hostility and aggression they would like to vent upon the unfortunate child himself. A child with a deeply seated emotional problem or with a physical defect may not be as well accepted as the teacher thinks he is. This kind of treatment is most likely to happen in the first three grades. Such a reaction may occur, also, if the child is the only member of a minority group present in the class. Later, the children may be considerably more receptive, providing the teacher has kept well abreast of individual and group socioemotional patterns and has tried to understand and further acceptable ones.

One highly respected and dearly beloved teacher, who perhaps seemed a bit old-fashioned even in her day, used to spend a great deal of time encouraging children to read creative writing of all sorts.[3] She established one pattern in early September, and adhered to it all year.

"Now, children," she would say very gaily, "when you see something bright and rosy-colored, how does it make you feel?"

The expected answer would come back, "Happy, good, cheerful."

Then, making her voice doleful, she'd say gloomily, "And if you feel out of sorts and unhappy, is there any color to describe it?"

"Blue," would invariably be extracted from the children.

"Now," Miss Whitaker would say, "let's pretend that each of us has a pair of rosy-colored glasses and a pair of blue glasses in his pocket. First, we'll put on the rosy-colored ones [and she would go through the motions] and we'll find everything good that we can, in what is to be read." A child would read his work and receive all of the positive comments.

---

[3]Miss Louella Whitaker, long a third grade teacher at the Midtown Ethical Culture School, New York City.

Then the teacher would say, "Fine, now put away your rosy-colored glasses [and the motions would accompany her words] and take out your blue glasses. Put them on [going through the appropriate motions]. Now let's see how we can help Steve with the parts that we did not like too well."

Steve would then receive all of the criticisms. While this procedure does not have to be used, it does point up one way to be constructive *first*. Having heard something positive about his writing, the writer finds it more easy to accept the negative and to find ways to improve what he has said. Although it is, of course, still a projection of himself, the writing has been objectified by his having written it, and becomes even more of an object with which he can deal after his classmates have evaluated it. The whole process does point up comments for the creator.

Much assistance can come from the teacher. The teacher who has built up good rapport will find it easy to say, "Well, which are you most concerned about or interested in, the fishing trip or Mrs. Jacob's parakeet?" Getting the child to verbalize usually helps to clarify the thing with which his feeling is most identified at that time. Another important aid in finding out just what the child is feeling is to get him to describe fully what he is seeing, either in reality or imaginatively. Then the teacher can be more helpful. For example, if, in a garden shop, the child is really so absorbed in the roses that he sees nothing else, then the teacher can help the child to express what he sees and feels by getting him to state it orally before writing. Others assist the child in expressing what he imagines. This is difficult because the adult must refrain from filling in the child's unfinished imagery. It is so easy to feed words to the child, groping for terms of expression, because the adult "feels" these belong to his song.

However, the teacher can be of genuine assistance, without either dominating or dictating. "Let's close our eyes, Ted. Now, you said that the hill was covered with snow and that a tall tree was on top of the hill. Tell me where to look for the den."

"It's under the tree," said Ted, "and the branches hang over it."

"I see it well now," answered his teacher. "Suppose you add a line, so that everyone will be clear about it."

Some children make finger or hand puppets for simple dramatizations or role playing. The puppets must be so simple that they are made quickly enough not to break the stream of the feelings and ideas which the child is struggling to bring out. The simple story, incident, or event is played out. The child begins to verbalize freely. When he stops, it can be written out more easily. If not, it may be recorded for writing later.

Other children know in general what their feelings are, but can't get started. If the child says, "I feel happy in the country. There are animals there, and I feel the sun." Then if he stops and seems unable to continue, letting him thumb through a book about the country or giving him a country scene or two to look at may afford just enough of a stimulus to get him started. Here, it is a case of focusing and clarifying feelings and of distinguishing those which predominate from those which are more peripheral.

The teacher must realize that children's sense of time and space is lacking, in adult terms, until they are age six and a half or seven. Things begin to be placed into historical and geographical context as the child clarifies the "here and now" and begins to develop the ability to push back in time and out into space. This ability also tends to be fairly well developed by age six and a half or seven.

The teacher can also utilize the kind of verbal competition that arises at certain ages as a jumping-off point for creative expression.

"My father is bigger than yours," said six-year-old Tony.

"Mine is. He's so tall, he's taller than a building," said Sam.

"Mine is the tallest. He is so tall that his head is up there hitting the sky," answered Tony.

At age six, such verbal competition is common. Getting the "taller than" recorded can be useful. The figures and images from such verbal bouts can be taken down. Later, the children laugh and enjoy the differences between reality and unreality. They are just old enough at this age to know some of the possibilities and impossibilities of their surroundings. However, the figures and images created can be, and often are, incorporated in what is written. The figures and images so created are likely to reflect the cultural milieu of the child and may be fresh and original formulations. For example:

> *It was tall as the fence around the project.*
> *It was noisy as that old garbage truck.*
> *It sounded like my landlord screaming.*
> *It was like a cow "mooing" after she left her calf in the barn.*
> *It was like a pasture I used to run in down south.*
> *It zoom like the plane came here from Puerto Rico.*
> *That boy just rolled. Man, I ax him and he roll like a big garbage can.*

Identification with image-making when the child is serious, non-competitive, and seeking to establish his own self-image is not the kind to be enjoyed with laughter. Gina said, "I am small. I am not tall. Perhaps I can be a dancing fairy. I can dance on a flower." Notice the "perhaps" and then the "can". Gina, struggling for positive identification, chose this form. An understanding teacher can encourage Gina to write this out, aiding Gina in objectifying her thoughts about herself as well as recording her developing creative powers. By third grade, such a child may write out a creative story of a trip to visit fairies, or some such fantasy, which shows not only her individuality, but her creative power. It also indicates her own self-acceptance.

One teacher used to say, "You've all seen the tiger in the zoo. Close your eyes. How does he look in your mind's eye? What is he doing?" Needless to say, the tiger was "doing" many things! Variations of a common theme of interest, such as the doings of the tiger as imagined by each child, can be very helpful in getting children to express the experiences they have had. In this way they are able to verbalize their inner feelings. Once expressed, judgment takes place and the individual subjective thinking of each child is incorporated. Again, we see that "writing my own story" is far more than just the physical act of writing.

A Brief Summary

Reviewing briefly what has been said, we find that:

Nonverbal expression of all sorts can be an excellent vestibule to creative writing;

Critical thinking is encouraged after the initial expression of feeling has been recorded;

Thought is to the feeling product what digestion is to food because the subjective must be objectified before critical thinking can be utilized;

"How" and "what" questions, asked within context, *after* positive rapport is established, can develop and clarify the child's projections;

Projection through an object held in the hand is often conducive to verbalization for a six year old as well as for a four or five year old, especially in a group setting;[4]

Utilization of a group theme as a generalized focal point drawn out of the particular expressions of individual children may further creativity;

Helping children, individually, to focus their feelings, interests, and ideas tends to make for greater depth;

---

[4]Occasionally, this helps a seven or eight year old, too.

Looking at one's own story in mimeographed form is helpful in
implementing grammatical and structural changes;

Individual choice, openly made, can be a worthwhile way to foster
creativity of expression;

Imagery is a focal point for self-identity as well as for creativity; there
is a reciprocity which follows to the advantage of each.

The teacher must learn when to talk to each child about his work,
how best to encourage skill in mechanics, and what type of encouragement is most helpful to each.

5

My House in the Country

*Some techniques for encouraging
creative writing from the feelings and
experiences of nine through twelve
year olds.*

In the years from age nine through age twelve the individual evolves
from the child who tends to manifest his individuality in the strength-
ened confirmation of interests aroused earlier to the pre-adolescent
whose fantasies merge toward roles of adult stature. "A house in the
country" can be the overt symbol of longing either for a settled
mature adult life or for a psychological refuge from a world too much
for the child!

The pudgy nine year old collects stamps with real concern, dreams
of being a great ballet dancer, or merely works along with his peers
in pursuing activities of daily concern. As he develops to pre-adoles-
cence, dreams of great deeds may occupy the eleven year old as he
studies about and identifies with knighthood. As she matures physically, the young girl of eleven or twelve fantasizes about princesses
from folklore or Hollywood extravaganzas, whereas at nine and ten,
she wanted to be an animal trainer. Immersion in imagery may be
healthy as a renewal period, but if excessive, it may indicate lack of
ability to cope with the problems of the child's daily situation. Socially, rejection wreaks havoc, yet too tight an in-group identification
can preclude the individual from reaching out! Throughout all of
these daydreams, healthy, unhealthy, balanced or immature, runs a

81

theme of identification with grandeur of person or fulfillment of some sort. The image may be the knight of the silver shield, the Florence Nightingale of the future, or the world's greatest ball player. These identifications serve as objectives to be reached and as symbols of achievement. The fantasies, dreams, and struggles serve as personal creative shields which frequently protect their originators and often serve as helmets against "hurts" from the problems of daily life. The rejected girl thinks, "Just wait until I am a star—then they'll see!" Or, "When I get to be a Captain, I'll be able to save everyone"—the boy's dream! Channeled into expression, the fantasies and dreams are avenues to creative writing. The reality and that envisioned, the "ought" and the everpresent "is," the dream and the piercing stab from peers are all fluctuating experiences which arouse expressions of self. As such, they serve as the source for creativity. When captured in written form, these feelings can be studied and judged by the writer himself. While judgment at this age level may be rash, it may, also, result from clear thinking on the part of the child.

In order to catch the feeling, connect the longing, and objectify the image for surveillance, certain techniques may be used. Each tends to focus the feelings of some children more than others, although few children are completely unresponsive to any of the following. As each child is an individual, so each responds uniquely, but all can be helped to write creatively about how they feel. Thoughtful evaluation may and usually should follow. However, in order to have something about which to think, feelings need to be expressed. When centered and channeled through nonverbal communication, written expression is merely stating what has already been expressed. In a sense it is a reiteration through a second medium of expression which gives enough concretization to feelings to let them be looked at more carefully. Reflection follows.

Several techniques, all suggestions usable with children from nine through twelve, are described in the rest of the chapter. Although practically every child will make some response to each one, each child will tend to identify more completely with some one technique or instance. For example, with "the house in the country," drawing is a step to creative writing. Illustrations involving drawing, music, lights, and pictures as well as other more familiar techniques are described. For some, these will be definite aids, while others will be able to write creatively without any preliminaries. However, even these children can benefit from time to time.

MY HOUSE
IN THE COUNTRY

"There," said Fredda, as she laid down her red crayon, "that's the way it is." She smiled as she looked at her drawing of a pale green house. There were bright flowers all around it and a tall tree—unmistakably a fir—to the right of the house. The windows of the house seemed to smile at the blue sky and the golden sun. In a few minutes, Fredda was explaining to Miss Shields, "You see, when you asked us to think of what made us *very* happy, I thought of this. It's where I was last summer. My house in the country makes me so happy. I smile inside when I think about it."

"Do you know exactly why it makes you smile inside?" asked Miss Shields.

Fredda was quiet a minute. Then she said, "Well, one reason is that it is so quiet. When it is quiet and there are flowers and birds, too, I feel good way down inside. No noise, no one shouting, and I am happy."

"Yes," said Miss Shields, "shut your eyes a moment. Imagine your house as carefully as you can. You feel happy, you said. Be quiet a moment, and then pick up your pencil and try to write about your house in the country and how and why it makes you feel happy."

Miss Shields encouraged each child as an individual. Her treatment of Tom differed considerably from that given Fredda.

"Bang, bloop, he's dead. Haa . . . That makes me happy," Tom said loudly and belligerantly. "I'd like to shout! Kill him! Watch him fall," he shouted.

"How does that make you feel, Tom?" asked Miss Shields.

"Good, great! I'm King of them all," snapped Tom.

Unruffled by Tom's blood and thunder, Miss Shields studied Tom's picture. Two heavily penciled figures were pointing guns at each other. Further down the paper, one was stretched out and the other was upright with his gun pointed at the fallen figure. "You really show how this one feels, Tom," said his teacher. "He won, didn't he? It makes you feel good to win, doesn't it?"

"Yes," said Tom. "I can lick anyone when I feel good. It makes me happy."

"Write it out, Tom. Explain just how you feel. Why do you feel good, after he's shot?" pointing at the prone figure.

"O.K.," said Tom.

While Miss Shields was working in this manner with Fredda and Tom, the other children were finishing their drawings and beginning to write on the yellow paper. Miss Shields knew which other children would be likely to need individual attention during the next fifteen or twenty minutes. She knew, also, that others would have short conferences early the next morning because they worked best without any interruption during the initial writing. When spelling was requested, as it was occasionally, Miss Shields wrote the word on the chalkboard.

Although this was a creative writing experience, the writing followed the drawing. Sixth graders like these tend frequently to express their feelings more easily after they have drawn how they feel. The imagery of their feelings is focused and then caught. The picture in the mind is set down on paper.[1] For many children, this intensifies the image. Then it can be written about more easily.

For younger children, drawing tends to set down and focus feeling. While this purpose still does function with older children in the sixth grade, their drawing tends to intensify feeling. The picture is a target and, also, something felt about strongly. The writing usually goes far beyond the picture in what is created. It is as though one still focused a movie film for further explication and clarification. While this is not necessarily the case with every child, it is a worthwhile technique to use for combined expression or when creative writing is to be developed.

Nonverbal communication is an excellent precursor to creative writing. In the situation above, Miss Shields had asked the class to think about what made the children happy. This focused their random thoughts. By being explicit about *happy,* she introduced one general feeling. The specifics, of course, were the children's own because each focused on his own imagery. Then Miss Shields led the children below their everyday patterns and to the threshold of their emotions. They were encouraged to reach more fully into the feeling level. This is necessary for creative writing, and this particular technique requires good rapport between teacher and child. Otherwise the child—a sixth grader or a six year old—tends to answer in the way he thinks someone expects. Intensified feeling is necessary for creative writing. It heightens visual and auditory imagery and often causes words to pour forth from deep inside the child. The thrust into expression should come from below the superficial exterior and the everyday mask. The "good" child lets forth "bad" feelings; these

---

[1]Many of these examples are drawn from my own experiences, during the time in which I was Ethics Consultant at the Brooklyn Ethical Culture School.

feelings reveal his strivings, desires, and sometimes the causes underlying his behavior. While psychoanalysis is not the purpose, it is our aim to find out some of the ways by which depths of feeling can be tapped for the genuine creative act.

About a week after the experience above, Miss Shields said, "Earlier this morning I heard you say, Bill, that you *hated* to go to your aunt's house. Do you remember?"

Bill nodded, and Miss Shields continued, "We all dislike some things more than others. Sometimes we are asked to do something when we don't really want to do it."

As Jane nodded and smiled, she added, "I know, Jane, that you don't want to take care of Peter, your brother, every time that you are asked. We all do things or see things that we dislike."

While she was setting the stage, Miss Shields began to hand out sheets of paper. When everyone had one, she said, "Yesterday, Doug said that he hated dancing because he felt 'tied' to a space. Joan said that she didn't like to go shopping for dresses because she couldn't choose her own. I don't know why Bill doesn't like to go to his aunt's. Bill, think about it. Then imagine yourself there. List words to describe how you feel. All of you, take one thing that you dislike; concentrate on it. Write it at the top of the paper. Now, list the words that describe how you feel. Don't put your name on the papers." While the children wrote, Miss Shields carefully avoided looking at what the children were writing. She did, however, write the words requested for spelling on the chalkboard.

After about fifteen minutes the papers were all passed up to Joan, who was seated near the front of the room. In this way greater anonomity was kept. Joan handed them to Miss Shields, who read a few of the disliked things aloud and some of the descriptive words from the lists.

For instance, she read:

Baby sitting for my Cousin. I feel "crumby," like a fool, mad, ready to cry, like running away.

Going to Choir Practice. Nutty, squeaky, goody goody, like playing baseball.

Doing homework. Mad, time wasting, like listening to records, hating Math, ready to quit, ready to give up plans for college.

Going home late. I feel like running, afraid, I'll see a thief, I'll be knifed, I want to get home. I want to get to the next street light, crumbly inside, goose pimply, like water.

The next day Miss Shields read summaries of the lists she had made by putting similar situations or things together and then listing all the terms used by the children to describe why the situation or thing was disliked. For instance, homework, shopping, and babysitting were listed more than once. The descriptive terms varied and so all were stated together.

After reading these, Miss Shields asked the children to think back about what they had said they disliked or hated, and then to write out a brief description of what it was. After this, they were to describe in sentence form just how it made them feel and why.

About a week later, the children were asked to think about something that made them feel very strongly—so strongly that they wanted to do something. Miss Shields carefully avoided reference to any specific feeling. The children were then asked to describe what this last thing was, and then exactly how it made them feel. Thus they were able to select and choose from among strong feelings. Lastly, they were asked to write out just what it made them want to do.

The results varied all the way from fear of ghosts to "feeling cool water run between my toes." The words describing the feeling ranged from "feeling eight feet tall" to "feeling like slinking into a mouse hole." The actions desired spread in a wide spectrum from "killing it with my hatchet" to "wanting to keep it in a small pink velvet box forever." Some strong emotional feelings of liking and hating reappeared. However, many other feelings, such as envy, fear, and the desire to emulate, were expressed. The children had gained experience in using words to express their own inner feelings. They had written creatively.

Thus we have three different situations from one sixth grade class. Similar learning experiences can be carried out with fourth and fifth graders. There will, of course, be some variation in what is liked and disliked.

The technique of stimulating children to feel strongly enough about something to express it in pictorial form is not new. After all, nonverbal communication was used by the cave man! Miss Shields, it may be noted, centered on a child's expressions of feeling in one situation in order to focus and to intensify the feeling. In another, she asked the children to think about something about which they felt strongly. Drawing, painting, using clay or finger paint are all means of projecting one's feelings outward. While one may feel a sense of well-being and be happy, in general, a particular feeling is usually generated by something specific. The picture focuses the real feeling and clarifies it. Once this has happened, the transition to words is often considerably more easy than if words are expected immediately. In the case of Fredda, talking or writing before she had captured the way she felt through drawing what caused her to feel this way would not have been very effective. Tom's hostility was so evident that words readily accompanied his drawing. However, had the image of his feelings not been represented graphically, the hostility might have continued and not had any release. In each child the feeling and an image were connected and a tension produced by the recollection. By expressing the recollection in representational form, some of the tension was released. Describing or otherwise writing about it stamped it more fully as the child's own, captured it for a more intellectual analysis later, and made the emotional experience more objective.

Miss Shield's method was actually simple. However, it could not have been utilized had she not earlier developed a relationship conducive to creative activity. She had established excellent rapport with her children. Each child was treated as the individual that he was which, incidentally, meant that some were interacted with at the time they were creating, while others were let alone until the process had taken place. She knew their individual needs. Too much talking at children, especially at the wrong time, can destroy creativity. Each child had learned, too, that any feeling was acceptable, granting that some control was exercised over overt acts. However, no "oughts" governed feelings during such times. With encouragement and acceptance, plus subtly guided continuity, release of expression was the result. The creativity was on a feeling level.

Miss Shields wisely refrained from being an amateur psychoanalyst even though, by her acceptance, she showed an understanding of how important it was to let Tom express his feelings outwardly. She did not reprimand, act shocked, or try to push any child into trying to express or repress some feeling as "right" or "wrong." The correction of grammar, sentence formation, and spelling would take place later. By her means, Miss Shields got the children to express what they really felt. What was created was the outer expression of the child's own inner feeling!

On their part, the children were able to achieve the release and satisfaction which accompanies true creativity. The atmosphere of acceptance was assuring. Each had found that his own individual feelings were accepted for what they were, and that to dislike something strongly, even to hate it, was a feeling common to all sometimes. Miss Shields incidentally tried to keep such feelings diverted from specific personalities unless they were deep and genuinely troubled the child. The children were encouraged, at such times, to keep their focal points unnamed. During other discussions about relationships, the anonymous centers of like or dislike can receive consideration. For instance, a principal or another teacher may be centered upon. If this occurs, it is usually wisest to let children talk this feeling out fully. Sometimes adult interpretation or even a meeting with the individual in question is helpful. When it is a political figure or some other publicly known person, children should be encouraged to ascertain the facts once they have written out how they feel.

I HEAR MUSIC

Mr. Berg had a very slow fifth grade in his inner city classroom. For some of his children, English was a second language. Writing was anathema for them. Any kind of response associated with the ordinary classroom was practically nonexistent. Mr. Berg had tried to meet the challenge and did carry out creative writing experiences in his classroom.

"Tyrone," said Mr. Berg, one morning after everyone had been seated, "You are tapping your pencil. Can you do it a bit louder?"

As Tyrone did, Mr. Berg clapped softly in the same rhythm. Several other children joined in. Some nodded their heads slowly, and somewhat lethargically, in time to the tapping and clapping.

"Listen," said Mr. Berg as he placed "Jamaica Farewell"[2] on the record player. Harry Belafonte's voice in the simple but definite rhythm drew some nodding and more pencil tapping. One or two children sang along softly, barely audibly. Mr. Berg watched, and as the movements grew more pronounced, he motioned with his hands for the children to get up. Some, more completely identified with the rhythm, began to move slowly up and down the aisles between the rows of nailed down desks. The slow but definite beat and the quiet movement of the children grew until all but three or four were moving around the room. Those at their seats all showed some response to the rhythm, either with head, feet, or hands. The children who moved around the room circled, shuffled, bounced, and some met occasionally and twirled each other around. The room had become alive, although the only voice heard for some time was the recording of Belafonte's. At the midpoint of the second playing of the record, several children joined quite audibly. One child muttered, half to himself, "Man, what a beat!"

---

[2]Harry Belafonte, "Jamaica Farewell," RCA Victor record 4470324.

Mr. Berg stopped the record and said, "Most of us have never been to Kingston town, but we feel something as we move. In your notebooks, suppose you put down 'I feel' and then how you feel, what you imagine, or anything you wish."

As he spoke, Mr. Berg's voice was soft but firm and precise. He had helped to create a mood which he did not want to destroy. He had watched nonverbal communication develop from a pencil tapping, of which the child was only partially aware, to overt rhythmic expression. He had observed that every child had responded in some way and watched as a few children interacted together through clasped hands or twirling. The nonverbal communication had grown from incipient rhythm to overt bodily expression. The music served merely to coordinate the children's inner beat and outward group expression. While other music might be suggestive, this recording was an accompaniment rather than a catalyst. As such, it kept the children's rhythmic responses constant.

The children, some still nodding, picked up their pencils and most wrote. Among their comments were:

I feel like I'm saling in a bote. Going to town.

I feel beat, beat, man I'm in a groov.

I feel like I'm in a erroplane.

I feel soft and I flote like on a rivver.

This was the beginning. Other days brought other records and other simple sentences. Mr. Berg had given the children "I feel" because he thought that they needed this much guidance. He had watched pencil and foot tapping and bodily coordinated response to a radio when the children were in the playground. However, they usually stood in one spot and moved as individuals unable to remain immobile rather than as creative children. Writing of any kind was a chore for these children. "I" was what the teacher wanted to develop—a self-image which could feel and then express what it felt. Imagery, as such, would come after the self-acceptance had begun to reach definition. "Feeling" is simpler than "thinking" because it flows out of one's present state; "thinking" would be harder and might not be the child's own in the kind of situation Mr. Berg had. "Thinking" would be encouraged later, after the feeling expressions became clear and identifiable.

A quicker, more confident and self-assured fourth, fifth, or sixth grade might have heard "Jamaica Farewell," the *William Tell*

"Overture,"[3] or "On the Beautiful Blue Danube."[4] These children would have been likely to sway and hum. In general, their responses would have been more immediate, but also more self-assured. How does it make you feel? What do you think of? Where are you? Such questions would have been enough to bring forth a variety of responses, some pungent, some flowing, and some hackneyed descriptions and images. A response to *Tales From the Vienna Woods*[5] for instance, might be:

> *I was dancing, gliding in the forest. Fairies danced near me and the moon's silver light made it bright. I drank in the moonlight and danced and danced.*

Here the child had identified rather completely and was describing herself as central in an imagined experience. The music merely stimulated her imagination and guided it in a certain direction. Obviously, possessing some self-assurance, she wrote down the descriptive scene as she visualized it. Another child:

> *The river sparkled in the sun. The fish leaped out of the water. The fishermen hummed a song and the waves on the water carried the boat along.*

This child imagined a scene and painted it in words as an observer. The results of being guided into one direction or another by the nature of the music heard can be restrictive or lead to greater outgoing creativity. This can be self-restricting, because the tendency may make an objective critic out of the child, which is fine in other situations. In a sense, he is object and subject all at once, because he is in his expression, which is objectified almost immediately because of the music. Thus, while the music and his feelings are identified, the music may have *initiated* the feelings. This experience can negate attempts to encourage him to identify so completely that he and the music and words become a self-enclosed subjective unity, which is objectified only when the words on the paper are read. If his feelings are present and are close enough to the surface to be the source of his own immediate identification with the music, then it is his own creativity which is expressed in the swaying and writing. This is comparable to use of the terms outer-directed and inner-directed in

---

[3]Gioacchino Rossini, "Overture" to *William Tell,* Finale, RCA Victor (ERB) 7054.
[4]Johann Strauss, "On the Beautiful Blue Danube," RCA Victor (ERA) 257.
[5]Johann Strauss, *Tales From the Vienna Woods,* VOXSTVX 426.030.

sociopsychological context. When the music has directed the feelings and been the outer-directing factor, the writing may then be more analytic because the self is not consciously made central. In this case, the self usually regains control and thus reclaims its inner direction, which is necessary before the second stage, that of reflection, can occur. Reflection unites feeling and thinking, on a self-directing basis if the action is to be considered genuinely creative. The genuinely creative work should be under the control of the creator.

Mr. Berg used music to build on because he had noted the rather spontaneous rhythmic responses and wanted these to serve to make overt some inner feelings. These were expressed by his children. Other groups would find writing less difficult. However, their responses to music are likely to be more varied and not always as immediately expressed in overt bodily movements. Definite rhythms such as marches, flowing waltzes, or polkas tend to induce bodily response. Some write with little overt bodily response to the music. Many sixth graders find that the words tumble out once music has stirred their feelings or helped them to create a definite image. Images tend to dominate their earlier writing; in some cases, real probing of personal feeling is necessary to bring the warmth of individual emotion to play on what is described. Stereotypes tend to disappear once the child's individual feeling is tapped. The stereotypic response may be so habitual that it will take a while to overcome it, of course, in other cases. However, when a child feels caught up in music, he lets himself go; and then the writing he does, comes more freely and easily.

THE LIGHT ROOM

Miss Kroger, Mr. Williams, and Mrs. Jansen, teachers of a fourth, fifth, and sixth grade respectively, had agreed to expose their classes separately to a similar kind of experience. Each teacher would treat the follow-up differently. They wanted to find out what, if any, carryover there was from the experience to creative writing.

The actual experience consisted of taking each class separately at ten o' clock in the morning down to the basement Light Room. Each class stayed about one hour. Here, in the Light Room, one of the art teachers had worked out a series of colorful, glowing, moving effects with a variety of lights, screens, revolving discs, and tables. After the room was dark, the lights came on in changing patterns and colors under the art teacher's control. A few of the combinations suggested specific figures, but most were conglomerates of kaleidoscopic color.[6]

Granting the age level differences of these middle level classes, each teacher took as a problem what, if any, extension of feelings or imagery appear in creative writing as a result of the hour's experience spent in the Light Room. Insofar as the teachers were able to ascertain, none of the children had ever been exposed to such an experience before this time. It was not a controlled experiment of any sort.

Miss Kroger's fourth grade was first. The light effects were in sets, each lasting five to fifteen minutes. After each set, Miss Kroger asked a) "How did this make you feel?" b) "Of what did it remind you?" c) "Close your eyes, what do you see?" This was a rather direct cause-and-effect procedure. Some typical responses were:

 a) *It makes me feel prickly; happy; like dancing; afraid, eery; slithery inside.*

 b) *It reminds me of fairies in the moonlight; a pool in the woods with fish in it; an acrobat in the circus; cool water; horses galloping.*

 c) *With my eyes closed, I see gnomes working at gnome work; a day beginning to be, and it came; a ballet with a princess dancing to meet a prince; ugly women sitting over a fire; a thief and a mugger slinking by; a horse ridden by a cowboy with a sombrero.*

Miss Kroger's children answered freely. Each of the twenty-four children tended to call out spontaneously, after each of the sets. As soon as the children had returned to their room, Miss Kroger passed paper and asked them to write out a short paragraph about something they had been reminded of by some of the light patterns and colors seen in the Light Room.

On the following day, Mr. Williams took his fifth grade to the Light Room, where they were exposed to the same variety of patterns and colors. Nothing was said during the hour except for chance remarks of the children. While these were not repressed, they were not encouraged. As soon as the hour was over, the children returned to their classroom. Mr. Williams passed out paper. He asked each of the questions asked by Miss Kroger, one at a time, and waited a few

---

[6]The Light Room was set up at The Brooklyn Center of Long Island University by Tom Douglas Jones, Research Professor. The three teachers and their classes are simulated from various observations and student and teacher reports.

minutes after each. The children were asked to write down their responses to the same three questions. The lists were very similar, with perhaps more responses from the boys. There appeared to be more variation in length of response. Some were rather hasty, as,

> *It made me feel cozy and warm.*
>
> *It reminded me of my cat and her kittens. I saw my cat and three of her kittens. The other was behind her.*

Other children elaborated to produce papers about as long as those written by Miss Kroger's children. Although no tabulation was made, it did appear that Miss Kroger's children tended to develop one theme while more of Mr. Williams' children tended to incorporate several items.

Mrs. Jansen's sixth grade saw the same colors and light patterns in the Light Room. The children went in, sat down, and nothing was said. After they had returned to their classroom, no reference was made to the Light Room. The children were given paper and asked to write out a short description of something which made them feel strongly. Mrs. Jansen found that several references were made to what had been seen. For instance, Henry spoke about the "The eery green light" which "reflected in moving shadows on the wall." Connie said that the children "danced like tiny bright lights." However, Peter wrote about cowboys capturing a wild stallion! Later on, Connie asked whether they might visit the Light Room again. Two days later when Bill wore a blue-green shirt, Alan remarked that it was the "color of one of those lights."

Although the real test of these activities would be what the children kept and used in the future, the exposure to the experiences in the Light Room, with the simple kind of guidance given by each of the teachers, appeared to add to the children's expression of definite feelings. It seemed to broaden and vary the imaginary scenes and patterns used by some. Individuals in all three of the classes made some mention of the lights later, and some children in every class utilized descriptive terms some months afterwards which appeared to have had their origin in this experience.

Although this was not research of a specifically planned, statistically evaluated, and carefully documented nature, it does give some preliminary experience for what could be a carefully designed experiment. It holds possibilities for focusing, deepening, and possibly extending the development and use of imagery by some children in three typical middle group classes. Lights—varied, colorful, and moving—probably give breadth to the feelings of some children and appear to help extend associations. For others they are probably instrumental in the creation of original imagery.

What needs further research, beyond the implications here, is a more basic question. Do the images utilized by children originate from them, from outside, or from a synthesis of both? This kind of experience is on a frontier which can be pursued and which may lead into research of genuine value in the understanding of creativity.

PICTURES[7]

Mrs. Lawrence had selected four pictures from magazines for use with her sixth grade. Each carefully selected picture was mounted neatly on white paper so that all would be alike and the color of the mount could not influence the overall impression. The pictures were chosen for total effect. She hoped that they differed enough to stir varied feelings. Two were colored and two were black and white. Mrs. Lawrence formulated questions which were to be used in an individual way with every picture in turn. After the individual picture had been looked at, the responses to the questions were to be jotted down by each child. The responses were to be anonymous if the child wished. When all the papers with the responses were in, Mrs. Lawrence held up the pictures again, quickly read some of the responses, and then conducted a discussion seeking to elicit further feeling from the children.

The pictures may be described briefly as follows:

1. A black and white newspaper picture of two starving Biafrans;
2. A black and white picture of a boy on crutches wearing a baseball cap;
3. A picture of a brightly colored bell held by a hand and ringing;
4. An illustration of a city street scene predominately, although not entirely, in dark blues and black. It is a quiet scene, but it is not clear whether it is at night, in rain, or both. No person is in sight.

The questions were as follows:

1. How does this make you feel?

---

[7] I have carried out these experiences while I was Ethics Consultant at the Brooklyn Ethical Culture School and have repeated them later with other groups.

2. What is going to happen next?

3. Why?

The responses are presented on the next six pages. Each of the twenty children in the class has been given an identification number which is used in all twelve lists; that is, child #1 in the first list is child #1 in each list. The children's spelling and punctuation are reproduced as in the originals. The children appeared to identify most with the first picture. It was referred to at various times in subsequent days.

PICTURE 1
QUESTION 1

1. It looks like they are very hungry and nobody will give them anything to eat
2. Sick
3. Awful gilty—nursus
4. Like someone is debribed more than I am.
5. I feel horrible and I never like to think about things like this
6. It makes me feel Discusting
7. Disgusted with the world
8. Sick
9. Terrible
10. Nourishs [Nauseous]
11. Horrible
12. Lucky we're not like that
13. Guilty, sad
14. Tired and sorry
15. Sick, it looks like Biafra!
16. Children starving in the world
17. Bed-sick weak-sad
18. It makes me feel sick
19. Sorry for them
20. Sick

PICTURE 2
QUESTION 1

1. It looks like its in Vietnam and he's in cruces [crutches]
2. Horrible
3. Sad, awful
4. Like someone is not getting the same advantages in playing as anything that takes walking or running.
5. I feel scared because it could happen to me.
6. It makes me feel that a good photographer took that picture
7. Makes me feel good
8. He looks like he is going to fall flat on his face
9. This makes me feel terrible, also
10. Like a pirate with a wodden leg
11. Horrible
12. Glad I'm not crippled
13. terribly sad.
14. Sad and sorry
15. Looks like Civil War or 1929
16. He's handycap
17. Bad and very sad   I feel sorry for him
18. It makes *me* feel handicapped
19. Sorry for him
20. Sad

PICTURE 3
QUESTION 1

1. People have to go to school
2. Happy
3. Wanting to draw, happy, laughing
4. Like great vibrations are ringing even though I know there is no sound.
5. I feel happy about this because I want someone to really ring it   Ring out freedom, peace, love, hope, justice, brotherhood, etc.
6. I don't feel anything.
7. Laugh-In News Sports
8. Reminds me of getting up in the morning
9. It makes me think about on a farm
10. George Washington and Paul Revar
11. Liberty
12. It seems like hereye here ye
13. Liberty. It makes me think of liberty and peace.
14. Happy and gay
15. Dinners ready
16. The sound of the bell is freedom going up to the sky.
17. Very good, happy glad.
18. I feel like my ears are going to burst.
19. Happy
20. It makes me feel like I have a ear aik.

PICTURE 4
QUESTION 1

1. A place to kill people.
2. Quiet
3. Sleepy-lonely-want to go home
4. It makes me feel like the lonelyness of the street would be stopped at any time by a man jumping out with a knife
5. It makes me feel spooked
6. Some delinquents are going to rob a store
7. Reminds me of a mugging seen
8. It makes me think of a peaceful street in the city.
9. Love and romance with peace.
10. Peaceful
11. Makes me feel scared
12. A quiet street in the night.
13. Gay but tired
14. Somebody gets mugged by mafia at night when everyone is asleep
15. Scary, quiet, lonely, afread
16. I feel like I'm going to be mugged
17. Scared
18. It makes me feel like I am in New York at night by myself.
19. [Unanswered]
20. [Unanswered]

PICTURE 1
QUESTION 2

1. They will die soon
2. Death
3. Nursus
4. Sick and weak.
5. They'll starve, freeze, and die.
6. They're going to say, "I'm hungry"
7. The whole world is going to come to an end soon.
8. The one sitting is going to lay with the other
9. They are going to die of hunger.
10. Start digging a hole
11. They will die.
12. They'll die
13. They will wake up
14. They will die unless somebody helps them.
15. They dye
16. They are going to die.
17. They will starve to death
18. They're going to get hungry and maybe die.
19. They will die
20. They might die

PICTURE 2
QUESTION 2

1. He will try to walk
2. Wanting to help
3. Like a very sad person because of his disadvantage
4. He'll fall unless he has a lot of strength and confidence
5. He is going to walk
6. Because he is recovering from polio.
7. Its sad
8. [Unanswered]
9. A reporter for a newspaper will take his picture for a newspaper so people will see that there are many handicapped children in the world.
10. [Unanswered]
11. He might walk.
12. He may be confined to a wheelchair
13. He might learn to walk
14. He will colaps
15. Sick
16. He will be able to walk some day.
17. He will never run or walk.
18. He's going to walk.
19. He can't walk
20. He might get better

PICTURE 3
QUESTION 2

1. Its sad
2. Ring
3. You might hear a sound
4. That a man is walking around yelling so and o'clock and all is well because I know in jerus they have a man walking around when they have he comes ringing a bell
5. If this happened then after its rung all would be happy and then there would be a holiday
6. He's going to hit somebody in the head with it
7. Big Al is going to say featurette.
8. [Unanswered]
9. Where the farmer and children are working and the mother rings the bell which means its time for lunch
10. Shot with an arrow
11. Its going to ring
12. Your going to hear a sound
13. There going to sign the Declaration of Independence
14. Children will come running
15. Everybody is going to stuff their face
16. [Unanswered]
17. All will be let free, liberty
18. I'm going to hear and see Avon Calling.
19. Calling people to church
20. Dinner is next

PICTURE 4
QUESTION 2

1. Its natural.
2. Noise
3. Shopping, writing something, like getting mugged, scared.
4. A garbage can falling over
5. Quiet and silence.
6. A bright light will, begin to flash
7. Somebody is going to get mugged.
8. Many police are going to come down the street
9. [Unanswered]
10. [Unanswered]
11. [Unanswered]
12. [Unanswered]
13. [Unanswered]
14. [Unanswered]
15. [Unanswered]
16. [Unanswered]
17. [Unanswered]
18. [Unanswered]
19. [Unanswered]
20. [Unanswered]

PICTURE 1
QUESTION 3

1. Because they are hungry.
2. because they don't have food.
3. They might die of starvation because they have know food
4. Because it looks like they are weak and sick because of hunger.
5. Because they have no home, clothing, or food and are badly handicapped
6. Because they are hungry
7. Because these people are neglected and life will be neglected too.
8. Examination of each other very carefully
9. Because they haven't had food in days and are absolutely starving
10. Because they don't have food.
11. Because they don't have enough food
12. Because they are starving.
13. They will be hungry
14. Because they look so sick
15. Because they don't have food too eat and clothes to were.
16. No food; cold, germs, diseases.
17. Because there starving (Their belly expands).
18. They don't eat because they don't have food

PICTURE 2
QUESTION 3

1. Because the legs are sick
2. he might have to get a wheelchair because he's criple and on cruthes
3. Because he can't do what some other normal person could do.
4. Because his face is full of terror
5. Because it must be a real boy to stand still in one place
6. Because somebody untied his shoelaces
7. Because that is what he does
8. Then, people will try to do something to try to help their children and he will soon recover not altogether but a little at least
9. [Unanswered]
10. He'll have to go inside
11. Because the doctors may not have a cure.
12. If he gets the right treatment.
13. The strain of walking
14. Somebody is going to kick his krutches and he is going to fall
15. [Unanswered]
16. [Unanswered]
17. Because he his cripple Something is wrong with is legs
18. Because he's in krutches and looks it.
19. Because his legs are hurt.
20. Because he is learning to walk better.

PICTURE 3
QUESTION 3

1. You're going to hear noise
2. The bell might come out the picture
3. [Unanswered]
4. Because the world would be a world worth living in
5. Because somebody untied his shoelaces
6. Because that is what he does.
7. [Unanswered]
8. [Unanswered]
9. Next everyone will come in and eat 'cause they're so hungry:
10. [Unanswered]
11. Because its being shaken
12. Because the bell is ringing
13. Because they want America to be peaceful
14. School
15. [Unanswered]
16. Cause Abe let all the slaves free, the fun begins very good Good for all children all over the world.
17. Because they need food
18. Because they's dopey enough to go around at 5 a.m.
19. So they know when church start
20. Because people use bells for dinner

PICTURE 4
QUESTION 3

1. I went home even more scared. What else do you expect on a dark lonely street.
2. Because there is not a thing moving, not a clothes line being pushed by the wind just nothing.
3. I don't know what will happen next. Because everything is calm and still
4. Because the muggers have nothing else to do.
5. [Unanswered]
6. They find out its a false alarm
7. [Unanswered]
8. It has to go home
9. Because its a dark lonely street the best place to be mugged.
10. Because it is getting
11. To attract attention
12. [Unanswered]
13. [Unanswered]
14. Because of the mugging in New York City, the gang and robbers in N.Y. City
15. Because it reminds me of a mugging.
16. Because its dark
17. Because it is late.
18. [Unanswered]
19. [Unanswered]
20. [Unanswered]

A quick perusal shows that there was the weakest emotional in-
volvement with the second picture. The child in the picture was
probably about eight years old and thus three to four years younger
than the children involved. The third picture was bright, and most
of the children smiled when they saw it. The pleasant association was
reflected in the responses. A rather direct action was to follow. The
last picture was the most provocative. Anxiety came to the fore. This
one seemed to arouse the most feeling, generally speaking. It seemed
harder for the children to make a conclusive statement about it. It
was referred to. Several children were heard to remark several
weeks later that it had made them feel "scary" and that one had to
be careful of muggings. References were made to places that looked
like "that picture."

Although these children were never asked to write out anything
further about these pictures, it is obvious that, having listed their
answers to the questions, they might have been asked to write out
what happened and why. If their feeling responses had been stirred,
the writing would probably have been at least as creative as the
verbal responses. Several children verbalized in some detail, especially about number four. Two got up from their seats during a
discussion of the scene and of what would happen next, and
quickly role-played their fantasy. Incidentally, each took the
aggressive role and then reversed roles and fell as the victim of
attack.[8]

This technique is worthy of considerable development. It would
appear wisest to encourage extension of whatever theme aroused
greatest feeling. Although most children indicated some form of
anxiety, several did not. To express one's feelings in writing is important. Sharing later may have a cathartic effect as the child recognizes
his deeper feelings more fully. In the expression, one may be really
creative. Creative writing, after all, is one's own and should express
that which is interwoven with one's deepest feelings. When one
picture appears to arouse more feeling than the others, however,
care must be taken to be sure that imitation is avoided and that each
child is voicing genuine feelings of his own. Needless to say, the
pictures must be selected with care. Clarity of image is important, as
is variety of mood from one to the other, if several are used. Three
or four, and no more, are recommended.

---

[8]This could be considered psychologically in some detail too.

OTHER AVENUES TO
CREATIVE WRITING

These techniques are all functional nonverbal entries to creative writing. While verbalism should not be rejected as a precursor to creative writing, it is my intent to stress the relationships between experiences, feelings, and creativity in various forms. There are other more common approaches which must not be overlooked. Several illustrations follow. In the first ones, the child lived through the experience himself. In the second group, the experiences were vicarious. In each case, the experience was expressed later with deep feeling by the child involved. First, let's take a brief look at the first-hand experiences.

Powerful first-hand experiences may be expressed verbally or in creative writing. Frequently no intermediate steps are required. For instance, a child's dog is lost. He grieves about it and becomes upset. Emotionally, his reactions may follow one of several patterns. In any case, his feelings are involved. Later, given the opportunity, he pours forth how he feels on paper. In some instances the teacher may ask simply, "Can you put down how you felt when something sad happened?" At other times, she may say nothing at all.

The experience of being locked in the basement of a school building with his teacher during a blizzard was quite an event for one of my pupils. He told about it with gusto the very next day. "How did you feel about it, Timmy?" was enough. He told about it dramatically and stressed his feelings of anxiety, of hope, hunger, etc. When the accident was discovered and the door was unlocked, his feelings changed immediately. Timmy was able to describe them.

"I heard a voice. It was up by the door. It was not an animal. Who would be there in the storm? When the door opened, there he was —my very own father. Gee, I was glad to see him." Later, Timmy told about the experience again; then it was written down.

In another instance, a four year old who set his own home afire was sent to pre-kindergarten the next morning in borrowed clothing which happened to be several sizes too large. At that time, he kept repeating, "There's a big hole there. It's black, all black." Later, he said, looking down, "Pete gave me pants. They're too big. Mine are all in the fire. They're all black now." My reassurance encouraged him to talk about the experience. Several weeks later, he referred to it:

> *I was remembering our fire and how scared I was. I think I
> won't make a fire again. They are bright, the flames. The
> engines made a terrible noise. They were like airplanes roaring
> down our street.*

Had he been older, this could have been written.

Vicarious experiencing, also, holds an important place in the lives of children. This is especially so of the older child who can read. He is able to identify, he has a sustained attention span, and he can literally live what he reads for long periods. Sections of *Call It Courage*[9] may grip a child. If sections of *Call It Courage* are read aloud, the reader can note how most sixth grade children feel the tension mount and then the relief when Mafatu reaches the shore and escapes from his pursuers. This, of course, is not as obvious when the book is read by individual children. A discussion of the book with sixth or even seventh graders indicates, in most cases, identification with Mafatu and the problems he had in overcoming his fear. Identification implies feelings, and these can be verbalized. The book lends itself to discussion which leads rather easily to verbalization of personal feelings of identification. Discussion should be kept general enough to avoid arguments over particulars. The discussion should provide a vent for expressing reactions. These are usually definite enough to create a mood. Verbal competition may arise as identification with Mafatu is expressed in terms of me and what *I* did. The teacher can wait until this has reached a high pitch. If the verbal competition centers around one theme, paper can be passed, while the teacher says, "Let's write out how we feel."

When the discussion and projections into personal prowess (or weaknesses) are varied, the teacher says, "Choose a time when you overcame your fear (or whatever) and write out how you did it."

The teacher can do this earlier, too. When the situation of danger to Mafatu is clear, she asks, "If you were Mafatu, just how would you feel, if you were being chased by the head hunters?" After the feelings are written down, the papers are collected. The next day, the teacher hands them back and says, "Let's all read these over for ourselves. Make any corrections that you think are needed." Having gotten feelings out and objectified, the children can begin to think about what they had said. The final paper might be different from the first draft, or the same corrected and polished.

Johnny Tremain[10] is another book with which children identify

---

[9]Armstrong Sperry, *Call It Courage*. (New York: The Macmillan Co., 1940).

[10]Esther Forbes, *Johnny Tremain* (Boston: Houghton Mifflin Company, 1943).

easily. Fifth or sixth graders tend to enjoy the first part, especially. The careful reading aloud of the incident describing the burning of Johnny's hand and the effect this has on his ability to earn a living are starkly real and gripping to most children. Identity again supplies the keynote to the creatively written expression of feelings. In this case, the results may express pity, despair, or hope. Discussion of ways to express such feelings should follow a first reading aloud. The teacher can encourage the children to express their feelings through description such as "I was there" or the "I was Johnny" technique. The latter is more directly revealing of identity and feeling, while the former, even though more restrained, may express anguish, for instance, as shown through bodily movement, words, or the reactions of others. Each technique, once objectified, is worthy of study as a means of communication.

A mood can be set, sometimes with poetry. The children's feelings are expressed in relation to the mood. For instance, the illustrations and the verse create a mood in *Spin a Soft Black Song.*[11] The feeling response by the child may be expressed rather immediately, or be carried about with the child as part of the experience from which later feeling may arise. His own later writing may well reflect his earlier feeling.

Often just reading a book whose leading character is an easy one with which to identify stimulates feelings which carry over. Sometimes twelve and thirteen year olds who have read *The Incredible Journey*[12] may write a story of animal adventures much later. If they have read or had read to them *Blue Willow*[13] or *Roosevelt Grady,*[14] they may begin the writing of the daily adventures of a girl or boy. Their own feelings are projected, and other experiences may be woven in. By the time the child is a fifth or sixth grader, this type of account may be similar to a diary in form. A certain amount of secrecy may surround it! For this reason, some of the devices for collecting poetry mentioned earlier may be useful.

THE ME

"Me" is expressed feeling! We have concerned ourselves with numerous expressions of feeling—of Me! Projected outwards, the expressions communicate to those able to listen. Identification with a

[11]Nikki Giovanni, *Spin a Soft Black Song* (New York: Hill & Wang, Inc., 1971).
[12]Sheila Burnford, *The Incredible Journey* (Boston: Little, Brown and Co., 1961).
[13]Doris Gates, *Blue Willow* (New York: Viking Publishing Co., 1948).
[14]Louisa Shotwell, *Roosevelt Grady* (Cleveland: World Publishing Co., 1963).

character such as Johnny Tremain may provide an outlet for one's own féeling in the projection. Role playing, which is considered in the next section, is feeling communicated through the spontaneous projection of "me" in a role. The role and "me" are identical for a time!

Interpretations: The Me Nobody Knows[15] utilizes feeling, empathy, and communication in a combined form. This record, filmstrip, and book set, made by youngsters, can be introduced after fifth or sixth graders begin to uncover the way they feel. It records the children's reactions to the book *The Me Nobody Knows* by Stephen M. Joseph.[16] This is somewhat intermediary between the identification with a book character, as mentioned above, and role playing.

Many educators as well as laymen responded to the feeling expressed in *The Me Nobody Knows.* The "voices from the ghetto" communicated clearly the feeling of black children. As the editor said, "These children of the ghetto, if given the chance and an open climate to write, have a tremendous amount to say and are anxious to speak."[17] And, later, "As you'll see, they are all trying to write what they feel, not what they don't feel." For instance, the eight year old who wrote, "I wish the My father will come back with My Mother. And I hope that whole world be peace and freedom"[18] does seem to express her feeling. She creates her world and identifies it with the whole world.

The Broadway presentation of *The Me Nobody Knows,* though acted, was done with genuine feeling. It was easy for most members of the audience to identify with the feeling objectified before them.

When the sixth graders read the excerpts from the book, in a related article, they created and presented their *Interpretation.* This was an identification with feeling expressed, but was more empathy than complete identity. The feeling was real enough! However, their identification reached the level of interaction on a feeling and thought level rather quickly. They experienced *The Me Nobody Knows* vicariously. Their feeling was in relation to this book—feeling in response to the expression of another. The feeling did seem directed to empathy with the other rather than objectification of the sixth graders' own expressed feeling. Thus they analyzed an object

---

[15] *Interpretations: The Me Nobody Knows* (New York: New York *Times* Book and Educational Department, 1970).

[16] Stephen M. Joseph (ed.), *The Me Nobody Knows* (New York: Avon Books, 1969).

[17] *Ibid.,* p. 9

[18] *Ibid.*

which was a combination of their thought and feeling interacting
with the ghetto children's feelings objectified.

"Now he feels left out and alone."

This was empathy analyzed by the sixth grader. Judgment came—of
the other, not of his own feeling.

"He feels that white people don't care about him."[19]

This is what the interpretor thought about the "he" and how he
felt! One wonders whether the children making the recording had
an immediate feeling response to the statement! Did they perhaps
react reflectively too quickly, and thus bypass their own feeling and
its objectification? This is an open question. However, the kind of
experience represented in the film strip and record and the interpretations, which were written and read, is an original and creative
presentation. It is provocative and has numerous possibilities!

WHAT ROLES
FOR PLAYING?

Dramatizing in almost any form comes naturally and easily to most
children. Dramatic play in the preschool and early grades leads into
more consciously sustained role taking in the early and middle
grades. By age nine, many children are adept at "living" as a dashing
prince one day, a lion tamer the next, and a cowboy shortly thereaf-
ter. Sometimes, however, one role is maintained over several
months, especially if the role is fed with new experiences. Role playing as a definite technique for expression, both verbal and psychological, holds an important place in many classrooms and should
function as a major means of communication.

If role playing has been established as a means of expression, usually at an early age level, it can be utilized more fully with the nine
through twelve year old. During this period especially, one's dreams
and imaginings are frequently interrupted by parental demands.
Baby sitting, care of younger siblings, household tasks, and pressures
exerted upon the child to do his homework may cause constant
friction. Role playing this "problem" story may be a fine opportunity

---

[19] *Interpretations: The Me Nobody Knows.*

for the teacher to help the child and class to better self-understanding. Writing these situations out can be a genuine creative act. The child's explanation of the problem, ways of overcoming it, the chosen possibility, and the action resulting from trying it out may show strong feeling, growing understanding, and keen intellectual insight. Encouraging the child to write such episodes in play form rather than in prose can result in creative dialogue.

For less articulate children, the open-ended story can provide an introductory phase for focus of feeling before role playing. It is wisest in such instances to obtain stories unknown to the children. "The Parsley Garden,"[20] for example, has several places which can be used effectively. If this is planned as an open-ended story, the reader might stop after the "older man" stops working—"Well,' he said"[21] —or after Al Condraj earns the cost of the hammer, and tells his mother—". . .'and Mr. Clemmer said I could have the job.' 'That's good,' the woman said. 'You can make it a little money for yourself.' "[22]

A point of climax should be chosen and the role playing started while feeling is high, identification with the story complete, and *before* the child can think out what to say. This is the only way to get authentic feelings in a role playing situation. The endings, too, can be written out.

THE AGE OF CODES, STANDARDS, AND PRECEPTS FOR BEHAVIOR

Children in the fifth and sixth grades often become concerned about codes and standards as part of the study of chivalry. Stories of knightly deeds appeal to them.

In one sixth grade, I read the Ten Commandments of Chivalry:

1 — to pray
2 — to avoid sin
3 — to defend the church
4 — to protect the widows and orphans

---

[20]William Saroyan, "The Parsley Garden," from *The Assyrian and Other Stories*, copyright 1949 (New York: Harcourt, Brace & Co., Inc.); as reprinted in *Counterpoint in Literature* (Chicago: Scott, Foresman and Company, 1967), pp. 4-7.
[21]*Ibid.*, p. 4.
[22]*Ibid.*, p. 7.

    5 — to travel
    6 — to wage loyal war
    7 — to fight for his Lady
    8 — to defend the right
    9 — to love his God
  10 — to listen to good and true men[23]

There was considerable discussion in terms of the specific items, such as "defend the right" and "loyal war," and just what each implied. The discussion was extended to include the consideration of codes, standards, and ethics more generally. Basically, the discussion seemed to revolve most particularly around whether behavior should be controlled. If so, what controls are necessary? How are they formulated? The children formulated their own Commandments (this was their term for them). Some selections from the commandments of some of the children, all from this group, follow.
    A boy:

> *Obey what you are told to do.*
> *Feed my cats when I'm sopposed to.*
> *Clean up your room without being told.*
> *Don't horse around at the wrong time.*
> *Be Good to Animals.*

Another boy:

> *I shalt not talk unless talked to.*
> *I shalt raise my hand.*
> *I shalt not hurt someone else.*
> *I shalt not yell.*
> *I shalt obey.*
> *I shalt not scribble on other peoples paper.*

A girl:

> *Do all my homework.*
> *Do not lie.*
> *Do not steal.*
> *Keep a clean and neat room.*
> *Be a good girl in school or home.*

---

[23]Elwood P. Cubberley, *A Brief History of Education* (New York, N.Y.: Houghton Mifflin Co., 1922), p. 91.

A boy:

> *Be clean and neat.*
> *Have peace between myself and other people.*
> *Be kind.*
> *Eat properly.*
> *Don't loose sleep.*
> *Do what your told by your mother.*
> *Don't make a move without thinking.*
> *Love.*
> *Fight for whats right.*
> *Take notice in what you do.*
> *Don't fight unless for a good cause.*

Another boy:

> *To protect people in need.*
> *To serve and do when told.*
> *To keep things of my own in place.*
> *Help when needed.*
> *Do to others as you would like them to do for you.*

One girl wrote:

> *I am satisfied with myself already.*

She had participated in the discussion in what might be termed a "goody goody" manner!

Concerns such as these at age eleven and twelve seem rather typical of certain middle class groups, who tend to be rather "ought" conscious at this age. Inner-city children often indicate the same concerns, but they are more frequently voiced and judged in terms of prevailing street codes. These often are tied in with attempts to break establishment regulations and to cut loose according to ability to achieve one's ends, even though these goals are not necessarily socially acceptable to society at large. Some regulations, however, may be in effect. One eight year old stole pocket knives to resell in order to pay for the movies. He did this for several weeks, but he only stole *enough* money for his specific purpose.

The attitude of middle class children often appears to be, "If I follow what is expected, I may be able to assert my own few concessions." The inner-city children seem to feel "If I don't accept this because it really doesn't apply to me, how much can I do actively to refute it?"

Many teachers in middle class neighborhoods encourage children like those in the first group to establish and to elaborate on their own individual codes, and then perhaps to elaborate more fully on one or two items. Many inner-city teachers try to establish enough rapport with children to guide them into some socially accepted formulation of at least one or two precepts for behavior. The knife stealer was given a job which netted him just enough for the movies, while other people sought to meet the basic needs of his family situation.

In considering behavior, teachers find that children in fourth, fifth, and sixth grades often find the fables of Aesop[24] and La Fontaine[25] especially appealing when they are used for a discussion of problems which concern them. Such problems as boasting, wishful thinking, difference, and listening to others are common. La Fontaine's *The Milkmaid and Crock of Milk, The City Rat and the Country Rat,* or the *Miller and His Son and the Donkey* are good starting points. Aesop's *The Fox and the Grapes* is also a worthwhile place to begin. Fables are short, to the point, and only require two or three characters in most cases. The animals and objects are simple and usually depict one major characteristic each. Many children are interested in finding out why Aesop used the fable form. When they do, they learn that Aesop wanted emulation of awareness of what might be done in a similar situation. He was using fables to illustrate moral precepts. The fact that the morals differ for the same tale in more than one edition can lead children to explicate their own versions.

An excellent procedure for creative writing is to list some proverbs or sayings, such as "A stitch in time saves nine" or "A rolling stone gathers no moss," on the chalkboard. If children are unacquainted with them, tell them a few others or get them to make up some wise sayings. Then inform them that they need two characters, one who follows the precept and one who doesn't. For example, the ant took a stitch when necessary and the snail did not. Now the children need to set up a situation. For instance, the mayor was coming to the village park, and each villager was to march before him. Now what happened when the ant did this? When the snail did? This kind of initiation by the teacher helps the children to see into fables. Many children then try to write some for themselves.

After these suggestions have been followed, it is frequently helpful, if the children are used to working in small groups, to divide

---

[24]See, for example, *Aesop's Fables,* V. S. Vernon Jones (tr.) (New York: Franklin Watts, Inc., 1967).
[25]See, for example, *The Fables of LaFontaine,* Marie Penset (tr.) (New York: Grosset and Dunlap, Inc., Publishers, 1957).

them and to let each group choose a saying and work out a simple fable to go with it. Some of these can be written down later. Many will take a modern turn and be quite applicable to present-day behavior.

A Final Word

The reading of poems related to interests, the taking of trips, and the encouraging of the individual writing creative verse have been considered in an earlier chapter. These, too, have an important place in the life of the nine to twelve year old. Although "The House in the Country" is typical of the nine to twelve year old, previously established creative forms do not disintegrate. Rather, they continue to develop and function on a more mature level.

The important point, however, is to remember that creativity manifests itself in various forms. It flows out of a context which may make itself apparent in many ways. While each child may have his preferred mode, all modes are interconnected. The nonverbal form is frequently more spontaneous. Utilizing such forms can provide an easier transition to the depths of inner feeling manifested through creative writing. This is often just as necessary at this age level as it is with younger children.

We have seen how different techniques can be used. The early ones indicate how progression can be made fron nonverbally to verbally communicated expression. The act of writing can precede verbalization, or can be recorded as verbalization takes place. Playing back and then writing can, and often does, act as an intermediary step, assuring that what is written is creative. Regardless of just when the creative writing takes place, it is a putting down of what can be stated as a result of aroused feeling which is stamped as "mine." Later perusal may, of course, add other dimensions as the initial expression is reconsidered thoughtfully. However, if each child is encouraged to catch and stamp as his own the surge of feeling aroused and developed by any of these techniques, he has a channel to creative writing. One note of caution: these techniques are not necessarily always worthwhile for every child every time. Each individual responds more readily to some sensory appeals than to others.

6

"Epidemic Hits Snails!"

How to record events, state facts, and review books while including controlled creativity.

Feeling, captured and recorded in verbal expression before it is thought about critically, has been stressed in the preceding chapters. Original expression should be the child's own creation! Too often, this is not so. Plenty of reflective, critical thinking is necessary after the poem or story has been set down.

Now, however, there is to be a change of emphasis! When "Epidemic Hits Snails," considerable feeling may arise after the fact is known. Facts precede feelings in record writing. Newspaper reporting and book reviewing are two types of record writing known to most children. Each can contain certain elements of creativity. However, each demonstrates a kind of controlled creativity which differs markedly from the kind of creativity we have been discussing.

HOW MATTER OF FACT?

Epidemic Hits Snails! The headline of the third grade newspaper was in bold, black manuscript. Direct and to the point, it caught your attention, wasted no words, and conveyed a message. The short hand-printed paragraph that followed told in concise, matter-of-fact

113

terms about the rapid decrease of snails in the aquariums in the third grade classroom. The snails, incidentally, were important accessories in the third grade project which was to furnish and service an a- quarium for any classroom that requested one. The hard fact, namely the sudden death of the snails, was an important one to be reckoned with in terms of the third graders' daily interests, needs, and activi- ties. It was important that all the third graders understand what was happening; that the event be communicated to them. This commu- nication had to be a special sort of writing.

One group of authorities divides children's writing into the per- sonal and the practical. The former is that in which the child ex- presses his thoughts and feelings spontaneously, as in the verse and stories of his own making. The latter is utilitarian and answers needs such as those for plans, memos, captions, lists, and reports.[1]

Although this distinction is understandable and to a great extent acceptable, my contention here is that the class newspaper and the book report illustrate a combination of the personal and the practi- cal. Certainly, both are practical in that the child must communicate effectively to some one else. At the same time that he is presenting facts, there is a place for his own persuasive terminology combined with his own evaluative skill. The two must be kept distinct in the teacher's mind. If a fire has burned down a building, that is a fact and practical. However, the way this is stated and any possible evalu- ations and hypotheses are personal and can illustrate the achieve- ment of considerable creativity.

The simple headline and short news account present a challenge to the young child which enables him to work out what is to be stated and then to state it briefly. Writing skills are less of a necessity if what is written is concise. The class newspaper and the book report both need consideration for their roles in creative writing.

RECORDING THE EVENT

Precision and accuracy are needed to record matters of fact. For instance, when fifth graders state that Baldy and Topper, the hooded rats, are the proud parents of six children, it means just that. Al- though there may be some question about a rat's feelings of pride, the two rats did have *six* children. If the babies can be counted, then the number six is an accurate fact. The rats did not just have babies,

---

[1]Alvina Treut Burrows, Doris C. Jackson, and Dorothy O. Saunders, *They All Want to Write* (New York: Holt, Rinehart and Winston, Inc., 1964). See pp. 2-4 especially.

they had six; and, furthermore, they were the offspring of Baldy and Topper. To the sixth grade, this was an answer to two problems: How many babies will the two parent rats have? How many babies did Baldy and Topper actually have after the birth took place? In keeping the problems before them, the children hypothesized and then checked for validation. Accuracy is the principal criterion for such recording and writing.

Poetic license has no place in the recording of factual events unless so labelled. If the facts are ascertainable, children need to face them and accept them. Creative embellishment which obscures the facts is poor recording and reporting. However, there is still a definite role for creative writing in recording facts and events. In the descriptive sections, originality and the clever turn of phrase are welcomed. One might say,

> *Topper came out of the nest and ate some pellets.*
> *She ran about before she ate.*

or

> *Flustered from recent motherhood, Topper eagerly gnawed some pellets.*

In the first version, the description of Topper is in the same matter-of-fact vein as the report of the number of children. In the second, the statement is more original. Both phrases describe what Topper did and do not obscure the fact. The second is written in a more interesting and original fashion. Certainly it is expressed in a more creative way.

The writer may go a step further and hypothesize that *if* Topper acted in a certain way, *then* certain conclusions might be drawn. In this kind of statement, the reader is alerted to the situation by a phrase indicating possibility and is assured, too, that this is the hypothesis of the reporter. For example,

> *I watched Topper. If she kept up that constant activity, she might melt away to a thin shadow.*

The teacher encourages the children to describe just how Topper is acting. "She is running," "she is scrambling," and "she is active" are typical responses. "If she continues," asks the teacher, "what may happen next?" "Melting away to a thin shadow" is certainly a creative use of language!

Biography and autobiography frequently re-create hypothetical situations.

> *If Amos had grown wings, he could not have attended to the wounded more quickly. He literally flew from one injured man to another leaving a pill here, a spoonful of liquid there, and a pat and smile of cheer everywhere. If the enemy had but had an Amos, their losses would have been fewer.*

In these last two instances, we have moved away from strict matter-of-fact reporting to a more original and creative presentation, which is to be encouraged as long as the factual information is clear and concise.

The classroom newspaper provides opportunities for concise communication. Writing a "punch line" for a headline is part of it. In doing this, children can be creative and original. However, they must not deviate from the facts, if good reporting is desired. The writer's hypotheses and personal assertions can be included but *must* be so labelled. Thus matter-of-fact, or practical, writing is writing in which the facts dominate. However, creativity in the way of presenting the facts, using phraseology and careful choice of words, is encouraged as means of communicating these facts to the audience. Creativity of approach, of idea, of the formulated hypotheses, of postulated conclusions, and the writer's analytic and evaluative procedures indicate unique intellectual creativity. In these instances, the creativity is a means to the end of an accurate, interesting, and concise presentation of fact.

CRITERIA FOR REPORTING

Prose writing of the matter-of-fact type is found most frequently in a school or classroom newspaper and in book reports. It is, of course, present in other instances, too. The child as reporter and book reviewer differs as a functional communicator from the child as a poet. Reports should be written according to certain criteria. These may be summarized as: emphasizing the facts as verified; being concise, interesting, and accurate; utilizing analysis and evaluation; limiting description to that which is precisely related to the topic. There is ample opportunity for creative writing after these criteria are accepted.

Emphasizing the Facts as Verified

What children think they saw, what someone said casually, and long
rambling sentences are out of place in reporting. Did the pigeon lay
two eggs? Was the flag at half-mast on *all* the government buildings?
What *happened* to the kitten? What *did* the fire *burn?* Such questions focus the children's attempts and result in such headings as:

> *Two Eggs Outside Our Window*
> *Government Flags at Half Mast*
> *Lost Kitten*
> *Garage Completely Gutted*

Now that the heading is settled, the facts in the article need to
meet verification requirements. Having verified the fact that there
are *two* pigeon eggs outside the window, the third grader can continue:

> *A gray and white pigeon laid two eggs. The eggs are on some
> paper and twigs. The mother pigeon sits on the eggs every
> morning. Sometimes she is away afternoons.*

The children had watched to see when the pigeon was on and off of
the eggs and had looked carefully at what served as a nest. Then one
child wrote about it. It is, of course, necessary to be sure that what
is written about and its title really belong together. The actual writing does not come easily to many young children, and physical
fatigue can lead to rambling accounts which may end up as something quite different from the original intent. If such accounts are
caused by fatigue, the child should stop. If he really has another event
in mind, it is best to let him sharpen his account and then to invent
a new heading or title. In any case, his account should be verifiable.

Being Concise, Interesting, and Accurate

As stated above, *Epidemic Hits Snails* served as the headline for the
daily newspaper of a third grader. The same individual, some twenty
years later, wrote, "Oasis in East Harlem."[2] Each of his headlines
focuses the interest of the reader; each is concise and accurate. He
has used what may be termed "disruptive association," a device
which children can develop. For example, "epidemic" causes one to

---

[2]Jonathan Black, "Oasis in East Harlem," *Saturday Review* (February 20, 1971), p.
52.

think of hospital beds. This association is disrupted almost immediately with the word "snails." The same disruption occurs with "oasis." Tall palms by a water hole suddenly give way to East Harlem. The device arouses interest! In each case, the author is creative in means he uses to present the facts. An epidemic is "temporary prevalence of a disease" and an oasis is "a place in a desert region where ground water ... provides for humid vegetation."[3] The fact is retained according to one definition and given an association which disrupts what is expected in the statements which follow.

The very nature of the heading causes one to want to read further. Children enjoy practicing this. How can we catch interest, be factual, and yet be precise?

"Magic Dust" and "In the Wintertime" were headings written by a fifth and a third grader respectively.[4] Both discuss snow and winter. Headings like the first can be developed by getting children to focus on a happening. "How do you feel? Can you see it or touch it? Is it like something which we all know or imagine? How can you make this real to someone else?" The concise heading can be presented creatively and yet be factual at the same time. "Dancers, Masks, and Drums" is the title used for a brief report by a fifth grader.[5] There are no excess words and the reader knows what he will read about. Writing a long headline on the chalkboard can be helpful. It can come from the children, such as: "Our Trip to the Museum of Natural History." In order to make a short, interesting headline, the teacher asks: "How can this be said in five words or less?" This can be a real challenge. Is it the trip that is important, or is what was seen of major importance? "Tepees, Tomahawks, and Canoes" was the result of one such experience in learning how to write interesting, accurate, and concise headlines.

Thus the use of disruptive association is one means among many to use in creating a concise, interesting, and accurate headline. The challenge of a word quota is another. In third and fourth grade, these activities may lead to much merriment along with the intellectual and creative effort involved.

Utilizing Analysis and Evaluation

The sixth graders who wrote signs, headlines, and articles about the Biafrans tried to analyze the situation from the information available in the library, on TV, and in the newspapers. "Children Starve in

---

[3] *The American College Dictionary* (New York: Random House, Inc., 1965).

[4] *Forty-Niner,* student publication, Brooklyn Ethical Culture School (June, 1969), p. 3.

[5] *Ibid.,* p. 16.

Biafra" and "No Money for Starvation" were two headlines. These were followed by quotes from the New York *Times,* the New York *Post,* and TV channels. The library was useful primarily in locating the country. The situation was analyzed as completely as possible. Data were collected. Obviously the children seemed to be starving. The sixth graders' conclusions turned into directives which were in essence their evaluations and recommendations about the problem. The evaluations could be classified into two major categories. Either "We have so much to eat and they have so little, and therefore we (or you) should contribute," or "Various groups are preventing food from reaching the children and we (or you) must protest this." The approach in such writing must be direct. In most cases it was. The descriptions of full versus empty bellies received much attention, too, as:

> *Here in Brooklyn, we all eat a big breakfast. In Biafra, the children have nothing to eat. This makes bellies stick out. You must help feed the Biafrans.*

When a visitor inquired of the children how they knew about this, they produced accounts, clippings, and quotes.

Limiting Description

Children tend to let their thoughts wander after their feelings are aroused and articulated. Occasionally, they associate freely. This tendency is to be furthered in poetry and imaginative prose writing. However, in news writing, the description should fit the object. For instance, the headline *Garage Completely Gutted* was followed by a description:

> *Smitty's Garage was all burned. A tow truck was inside. It was all black. Even the gas pumps outside were black. Smitty's coke stand and some empty cans were bent from the heat. The garage was gutted.*

The teacher encouraged focusing on the particular fire which burned Smitty's Garage. Young children sometimes generalize, such as, "Fires burn everything" or "Fires are dangerous." While true, these statements have nothing special to do with the particular fire at Smitty's Garage. Children also tend to bring in their own other experiences which deserve consideration, but usually do not add to such factual reports as that about Smitty's garage fire. Specificity is important; details should relate to the particular situation.

THE BOOK REVIEW

The book review expresses factual information, some analysis, and some evaluation. Like the child's news item, the factual part should give an accurate account. For example:

> *Pasteur discovered the main cause of diseases, germs or small organisms, and developed cures.*[6]

certainly gives a factual account, while

> *This book taught me never to give up on something I begin*[7]

and

> *Answers will come for everything someday, we hope, through research and increased knowledge*[8]

indicate some personal analysis and evaluation.

While the child can read the book and then write out what it is about, he can also be led to a more creative approach to it. Book reports are written to indicate to others something about a book which may interest and inform them. The child's response should be factual, but creativity and feeling may enter also. For instance, the child could write

> *The author made me feel as if I lived in New Amsterdam.*

or

> *Wouldn't it have been strange to have lived in New Amsterdam! Just imagine the Dutch ships coming and going!*

When the child steps beyond the completely factual account, he may imagine himself in the situation. Identification helps analysis.

> *Peg Leg Stuyvesant stumped down to the wharf, like the ruler of all he surveyed. I think he felt very proud of New Amsterdam. I would have.*

Upon being asked what it feels like to be left behind, the child adds to his reasoned approach when he tries to describe the same situation

---

[6] *Ibid.,* p. 20.
[7] *Ibid.*
[8] *Ibid.*

in a book. Both feeling and thought interact with the facts in the book.

> The knight felt sad, but he had to do his duty. He was a responsible knight. Responsibility is sometimes very hard, I think.

Identification with a character may lead to other forms of creative writing, too, of course. However, seeing through the eyes of another gives a sense of reality which makes analysis easier.

Encouraging children to pick out the highlights may encourage an enthusiastic flow which builds up. What was the most exciting part?

Using onomatopoetic phrases, pungent words, and playing with words all make the report a more creative enterprise. "The sagging door creaked in the breeze," written by a fifth grader, says more than the bare fact alone. The second grader may go around chanting "saggy, baggy, saggy, baggy, paggy, maggy" after his little brother is seen with *The Saggy Baggy Elephant.*[9] Later, he uses the phrase, "The man was old and wore saggy, baggy pants."

Thus it is evident that the book report, like the news article, is a place for some creativity in writing controlled by the facts given. Such controlled creativity adds a spark to a report which should not be only related strung out sentences. A book report can be exciting. It can be written creatively. After the facts are ascertained, feeling and thought interact with the facts. However, the facts in the book regulate what is said.

TEACHER'S ROLE

The teacher's part in guiding the newspaper reporter and the book reviewer differs somewhat from her function in a completely creative situation. News items and book reports are primarily matter-of-fact practical items. Therefore, accuracy must control what is said. However, after the governance of this primary criterion is clear, creativity can function effectively in other important ways.

Briefly, what the teacher endeavors to do may be summarized as follows:

Stress the necessity for an honest recording of the news event or of the contents of the book. This is primary. In conjunction with it,

---

[9]Kathryn Jackson and Byron Jackson, *The Saggy Baggy Elephant* (New York: Golden Press, Western Publishing Co., Inc., 1952).

the multisensory approach should be encouraged: what did you see and hear; how did you feel; what did it make you want to do, etc.

Urge children to search for the answer to why or how the event happened or for the purpose for which the book was written. It helps children to clarify a problem for which to collect their facts. Since each child is a unique individual, his means will differ, and his own way of looking at the event or purpose will be reflected in his factual account. Careful observation is encouraged.

Encourage each child to imagine himself as the audience and to decide what questions might be asked of the reporter or reviewer. The transposition of roles adds understanding and encourages clarity of communication.

Work with individuals, orally, and with the class as a whole. Use the chalkboard in order to practice headline formation. This is often fun for the children and opens up a creative avenue for each one.

Leave time for each individual (or for those involved) to write his own headline after a number of their samples have been written on the board by the teacher. While they are ready and enthusiastic, they can write. If they begin before samples have been placed on the board, they may find the writing fatiguing and lose interest. Fifth and sixth grade children, of course, may be ready to write before younger ones.

Stress the need to pique the curiosity and interest of the reader by the careful choice of words. Here is the chance to encourage a factual yet original and colorful use of words. For instance, what words may be more expressive than "hanging down," than "place," or than "Indian homes?"

Limit the number of words to be used (occasionally). For example, ask who can write the most informative and interesting headline or title using only five words (the headline should be about a specific event and the title about a specific book).

Focus on creativity in depth of expression rather than breadth. Onomatopoetic or descriptive words add to the interest in a headline or a title. In the account or book report, depth of expression can be encouraged by questioning just what is indicated by certain words. For instance, if Abe Lincoln was a kind man, what indicates this? Are there a few words which tell this concisely? Thus concise description may utilize words in original combinations.

Encourage reading to each other. This is helpful because audience reception is necessary. Do you, as the listener, want to know more about the news item? Does his report cause you to want to read, or not read, the book?

Teach dictionary skills, some punctuation, synonyms, and spelling, in terms of age level, as concomitant skills. They can be understood as requirements which arise from the necessity to communicate the material clearly.

Encourage the writer's own hypotheses and evaluations. These must be distinct from the objective, matter-of-fact report. Older children begin to clarify between the objective and the subjective; for example, "if such fires happen often, the neighbors may need to help" and "the book made me want to plan how to teach my dog how to pull me on a sled." After the fact is stated, the individual's own feelings and thoughts interact with it. This is not to change the fact, but to present it well and to make the means of analysis and the evaluation original. When possible the individual's projections, clarified as such, do have a place. These may utilize considerable feeling.

Summary

Facts and feelings! It has been said that feelings are facts. While this is so, subjectively, a burned out garage is an ascertainable, verifiable, objective fact. Given a creative teacher, however, the objective fact can be one part of a child's presentation. The child also can express feelings which are subjective in certain ways. Each has its place in the recording of a news event or in the review of a book.

7

Finale? No, Only a Beginning!

The consideration of feeling, thinking, reformulating, and learning skills in terms of general expectations and specific objectives.

FINALE

A quote from one of Hentoff's characters provides a worthy note for a finale. Hitchcock, the bass player, says, quoting a colleague, " 'Music is your own experience, your thoughts, your wisdom. If you don't live it, it won't come out of your horn' . . . When you're improvising, man, you're going inside your*self* to dig out how *you* feel at that moment, and if you haven't lived enough to feel enough, you're not telling any kind of a story that's worth hearing."[1]

If you substitute "creative writing" for "music" and "pen" for "horn," the statement is pertinent here. Everyone needs to look in, to be able to express his feelings in ways that communicate to others. When written, this is creative writing. Let's encourage children to dig out how they *feel*—set it down, think about it, perhaps rewrite it. Let's let them write creatively!

Finale? No, only a beginning! The preceding chapters contain convictions and general objectives as well as suggestions for achieving them. The convictions are my own. They are derived from years of

---

[1]From JAZZ COUNTRY by Nat Hentoff, p. 16. Copyright © 1965 by Nat Hentoff. Reprinted by permission of Harper & Row, Publishers.

experience and from reflections upon that experience. They have been derived from trying out, thinking about the results, and trying out again. They represent projections which, in many cases, have reached some measure of realization. Ends for future activity need to be formulated on the basis of what has been achieved first and from consideration of what can be achieved second. Goals of realization for self and society should be based upon what is, derived from what was, combined with what can be. Pie in the sky? No, aims should be possible to achieve within a forseeable future. Aims must be flexible enough to meet necessary needs for reassessment, for reformulation. What was has given us what is! The most useful and worthy of that "is," as I see it, is the base from which our future arises. We are all part of a continuity and it behooves us to assess it. What can we do to match our achievements to our aims? Our wants and needs are involved, and our self-image requires certain fulfillments. Realization of the self and of the other requires such matching and such fulfillment.

This, of course, is general. Each of us puts in his own particulars without which we would not be individual. Though all of us walk, the place to which we walk, much of the reason for a particular walk, the way we walk and some portion of what is done after walking is specifically Grace or Alan. Much of the quantity of everyone's life is similar, but qualitatively, everyone's life can be individual. We experience some incident and reflect upon it. Problems raised push for our solution. We struggle to use the quantity of our past experiential data, qualitatively refined into the particular factors which we reformulate as data for these problems. We try out possibilities and continue on, or reconsider if the obstacle is still before us.

The specific experience which any man undergoes recedes into referential data for further experiences. New experiences may be mundane ones, with problems of how to unlock a recalcitrant door, or whether to go to the grocer's before or after the bank. Other events, less mundane, arouse—or can arouse—immediate feeling. A man is hitting a child, and we feel immediate anger. Sibelius' Second Symphony greets our ear as we enter a building and an immediate feeling of happy accord with a majestic northland pervades us. If we accept the feeling for what it is in each case, we have made an object of it, and can decide reflectively what to do about our own subjective feeling.

As adults, we do frequently respond with feeling which is so immediately objectified that we can think about it right away and make a decision. However, children do not usually react this way. The very young child can think reflectively, but he can and does feel, too. Too often his thinking is based not on experiential data of his own functioning, but on cultural habituations. They are usually derived from the very small cultural segments which impinge most directly upon him. He has learned, all too often, to reject his own feelings and any later reflection on them as objects. Instead, his data have become "What will she like?" In order to live in society, of course, some social habituation is necessary. But in order to live as an individual, the personal subjective feeling element is a necessity! Balance between personal and social requirements is necessary.

This means that each child must have opportunities to judge and reflect upon the objectification of his own feeling. He thinks about it after it has become an expression or object. Then his thoughts and feelings interact and he does whatever is necessary.

Many years ago, I visited a Children's Zoo. It was one of the first in the country and had only been open for about a week. Many domestic animals wandered freely about the place. A small boy, about four and a half or five years old, was squatting on the ground, vigorously patting a large and docile rabbit. But the boy was not looking at the rabbit. Instead, he was staring at a woman and screaming, "See me! See me! I am being *interested* in the rabbit!" How many compositions, written in our schools, really read under the surface "See me! I am being interested in the—whatever you say or think is important."

Feeling expression is necessary to creativity. Four year old Steve picks up two blocks and claps them in a rhythm which expresses his own feeling. No one else in the nursery class is aware of this at first because everyone is busy at his own work and play! Others join him later, and the teacher plays a march to accompany what Steve is doing. Soon the whole activity has ended. In the second grade, Steve is watching the mounted policemen from the window. He moves his hand up and down. He says,

> *Clip, clip, clop,*
> *Clip, clip, clop,*
> *Horses, shining like my new pennies,*
> *Make their shoes sound*
> *Like a parade marching by.*

The Steves and Jennies, Sols and Sarahs, Marias and Juans have the right to see horses like pennies. And the adults around them have the obligation to accept these creative expressions of feeling caught and set down for consideration.

Feeling is expressed through many kinds of creativity. Rhythm or pattern seems to be a universal base. Creativity of one type is related to that of another. Thus Steve clapped blocks at one time, expressed the rhythm of the horses with hand motion, and then expressed it verbally. If he had been older, creative writing might well have been the initial verbal form. By separating, or seeking to separate, one objectification of feeling from another, creativity is often maimed, especially with very young children. With older ones, the relationships frequently show themselves when the atmosphere is open and free enough to permit innovations. What a far cry from, "Now, children write a story about the fall season." With all due respect to autumn, let's let children express how they feel! Caught in written form, this is creative writing.

THE ROLE OF PARENTS

What of parents who push instead of listening and recording? Perhaps they need to listen and to accept their own feelings. Then they may respect the feelings of their children. Only the rare parent records his child's "special" statements. The special event and David's wonder, expressed in his own way, is his own particular creativity. The mother, who read such statements to her child occasionally at bedtime sent him happily to sleep. "Do you remember what you said about the baby rabbit today? You said he jumps and skips like a big grasshopper! His tail shows soft and furry. He is jumping so he can see the other bunnies."

Parents want their children to succeed, to achieve, to compete, and to win, when possible. Pushing them, putting words into their mouths, telling them what to feel are false conceptions of assistance. Parent responsibility means taking Sue and Sam where they are, deciding what is needed for further development, and seeking to supply it. What is needed may be someone to listen. It may be taking a trip to a special place. It definitely is someone to hear the child's statement when he "sees a glowing sunset."

The parent who speaks another language has the obligation to share with the child the gifts of that language and of the culture which it represents. The Cruz sisters, at ages four and five, could harmonize simple Puerto Rican songs. Their songs in Spanish were a delight to hear! Later, written words would express their feelings. However, they were accustomed to expressing how they felt. When Clotilde's hair was pulled, she screamed. Carmen to the rescue!

Later, in Spanish, Clotilde explained just how she felt to the assistant, who understood Spanish. Better to express what one feels in another language than not to express.

The understanding teacher will utilize the parents, regardless of background. The only requisite for a contributing parent is understanding and feeling. A certain language and social status are not prerequisites to encourage the kind of feeling expression which is a precursor to writing.

SIGN POSTS

Skills? Yes, but in their place. Later, after there is something about which to be skillful. Children who write creatively set down their feelings first. Judgment is next, and then usually a feeling–thinking reformulation. Periods and question marks are considered at this time. How can Jon understand the use of a question mark, if he has never felt a question?

However, you shouldn't just say "hands off!" Instead, take time: watch! listen! supplement! Answer to the need for quotation marks, when the feeling is down as I felt this and so *I* said it.

Objectives? Sure, for each in terms of where he is specifically, and in the context of general expectations for the group! General objectives for clear written communication are the sign posts on the road of creativity. If you don't start down the road, the sign posts are useless! If you have a number of sign posts first, they are debris in the path of setting out on the road. Until you experience what travel is, you can't very well travel to a destination!

In sum, let's let them write creatively!

INDEX